THE NUBIAN
PHARAOHS

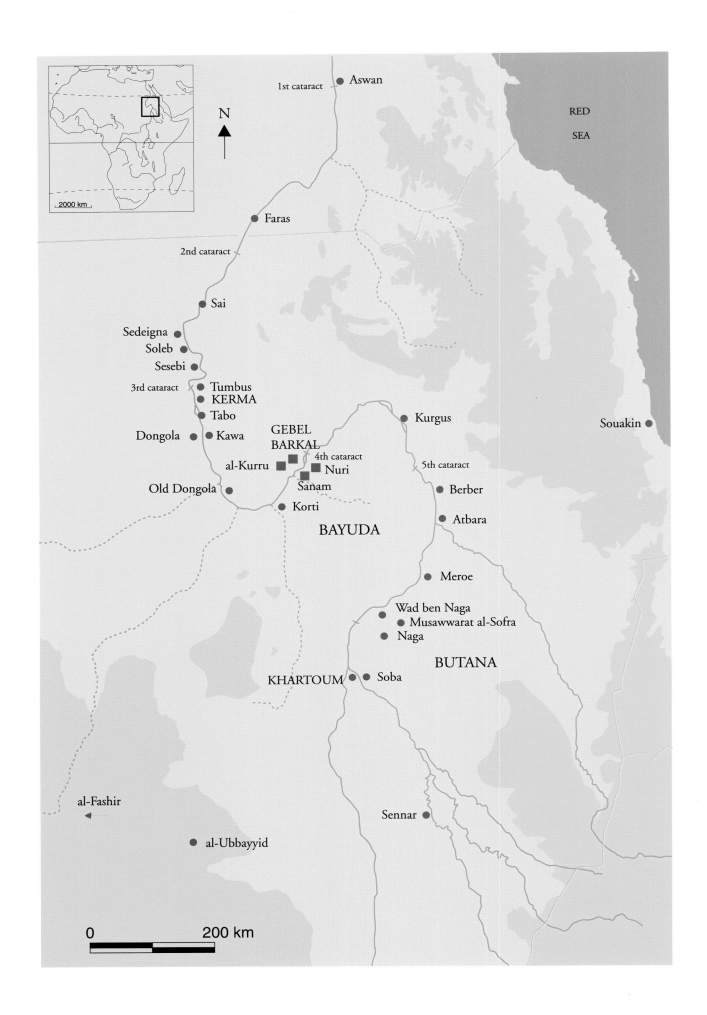

1st cataract

Aswan

RED

SEA

Faras

2nd cataract

Sai

Sedeigna

Soleb

Sesebi

3rd cataract   Tumbus

KERMA

Tabo

Kurgus

GEBEL

Dongola   Kawa   BARKAL

Souakin

al-Kurru   4th cataract

Nuri

Old Dongola   Sanam   5th cataract

Berber

Korti   Atbara

BAYUDA

Meroe

Wad ben Naga

Musawwarat al-Sofra

Naga

BUTANA

KHARTOUM   Soba

al-Fashir

Sennar

al-Ubbayyid

N

2000 km

0   200 km

Map of Sudan

Charles Bonnet
Dominique Valbelle

THE NUBIAN PHARAOHS

Black Kings on the Nile

Foreword by Jean Leclant

The American University in Cairo Press
Cairo   New York

CONTENTS

The bust of one of the two statues
of Tanutamun

Foreword

by Jean Leclant

The Nile Valley is constantly yielding new treasures. News agencies regularly announce new finds, though they may not always be from the major international tourist sites, or always of equal value. Following all the attention focused on Nubia in the 1960s (part of which disappeared beneath the rising waters of Lake Nasser behind the dam at Aswan) people became interested in searching for antiquities farther south, in Sudan, a vast region that still had not been thoroughly explored. A few archaeological missions were thus organized, notably one led by Professor Charles Bonnet from the University of Geneva. Bonnet's team started work in 1977 at Kerma, just upstream from the Nile's third cataract, where it unearthed a sub-Saharan type capital city, far south of Egypt. Kerma was a key town in Africa's first kingdom, Kush, and the site yielded finds that made it a modern center of international archaeology.

We should thus be grateful for the publication of *The Nubian Pharaohs: Black Kings on the Nile*. This magnificent book certainly deserves a special place among the flood of publications currently fueling readers' enthusiasm for ancient antiquities, as it demonstrates that, alongside Egypt proper, Sudan now constitutes an important realm of Egyptology. Readers will discover a cache of splendid statues—recently unearthed in Sudan—that are already ranked as masterpieces of art history. The accompanying text discusses various ritual practices rarely addressed in similar publications.

It was on January 11, 2003, that Charles Bonnet began to excavate a round, three-meter pit in Kerma, now called Doukki Gel, formerly the Egyptian town of Pnubs (city of the jujube tree), and a successor to the ancient capital of Kush. In that pit were seven statues—deliberately but carefully broken into more than fifty pieces—along with remnants of the gold leaf that had originally adorned them. Once reassembled, these statues constituted a magnificent gallery of kings, including Taharqa and Tanutamun, the last two pharaohs of Egypt's Twenty-fifth Dynasty (formerly known as the 'Ethiopian' pharaohs, now generally referred to as 'Kushite'). The two admirable statues of Tanutamun are

Head of one of the two statues
of Senkamanisken

7

the first to reveal his facial features. Taharqa, who ruled in the first half of the seventh century BCE, was the powerful Kushite king who long resisted Assyrian invasion and thus merited mention in the Bible. Finally vanquished around 656 BCE, the 'Black Pharaohs' were forced to abandon the lower Nile and withdraw to the south, thereafter reigning in Nubia as the Napatan Dynasty. Although the cache of statues found by Bonnet's team at Kerma, like a similar one found in Gebel Barkal, lacks a visual record of the first Napatan monarch Atlanersa, it contains sculpted portraits of his successors Senkamanisken (two statues), Anlamani (with an impressive ram's-horn crown), and Aspelta. Indeed, these tough conquerors from the south, with their strong features and powerful bodies, combined Egyptian royal insignia with more specifically African attributes, notably invoking their ram-god, Amun, who became a dynastic god of the Egyptians.

Authors Charles Bonnet and Dominique Valbelle have placed this recent, major archaeological find in its historical context by recounting in simple fashion the main phases of the kingdom of Kush (much better known today thanks to the work of the Swiss team at Kerma), which came to rival the great ancient civilizations. It began as a special culture that emerged in the late third millennium BCE, typical of the sub-Saharan environment in which it developed. In the middle of the second millennium, around 1560, there followed some five hundred years of Egyptian domination, thus explaining the presence of traces of Akhenaten's Amarna culture in those distant lands. Finally, a Nubian resurgence in the eighth century BCE enabled kings from the area called Napata (downstream of the fourth cataract) to invade Egypt. Led by the conqueror Piankhy, Nubian power in Egypt was consolidated by the first Kushite pharaoh, Shabaqo, followed by Taharqa— thereby raising fascinating issues of acculturation.

Given the royal statues found in the cache, this book stresses the Kushite and Napatan aspects of Egypt and Sudan, respectively; its lavish illustrations will allow readers to appreciate the talents of both Egyptian and Nubian sculptors. The individual features and characteristics of monarchs, who have now taken their place in history, emerge in an expressive art that combines the rigor of revived classicism with a fascinatingly 'primal' aesthetic. Certainly many budding Egyptologists—and Africanologists—will be delighted to find here unexpectedly concrete evidence of negritude. We are thus a long way from the purely theoretical speculation that once animated fascinating conversations about Kushite civilization that I used to have with President Léopold Senghor of Senegal, back when excavations in Sudan where just getting underway.

What is the true significance of the carefully broken statues in the Kerma cache? How do they relate to the ones found at Gebel Barkal in the Napata region in the early twentieth century, whose importance and uniqueness was overlooked? Their fate obviously has something to do with the Egyptian expedition led by Psamtik II in 591 BCE, deep into the heart of Nubia when Aspelta was reigning there. The hypotheses concerning the breaking of these statues, followed by the total conservation of all their fragments, still leave many questions unanswered. Scholarly interpretation can nevertheless progress through the examination—and re-examination—of other *favissae*, or ritual caches, such as the one uncovered at Karnak in 1905 (when Georges Legrain found thousands of statues and ritual objects by 'fishing' for them down to the level of the water table) and, more recently, in the temple at Luxor (whose splendid finds are now on display in a new wing of The Luxor Museum of Ancient Egyptian Art).

Egyptology is thus constantly enriched with new evidence, documentation, and food for thought. Yet even as art history is being enriched with new masterpieces—and the treasures found in the Kerma cache certainly merit that label—we are simultaneously forced to face questions that were previously overlooked. But that is how scholarship—true scholarship—proceeds.

The publishers therefore deserve congratulations for publishing a text that explores a new geographic realm and deals in scholarly fashion with issues that are far from resolved. I wish readers a *bon voyage*, for they are about to embark upon a trip to harsh climes, treacherous cataracts, and difficult roads, in order to discover the grandiose beauty of a sacred mountain called Gebel Barkal and the fascinating culture behind these newly unearthed treasures, which are soon to be exhibited in the new museum in Kerma.

JEAN LECLANT
Honorary Professor, Collège de France
Perpetual Secretary, Académie des Inscriptions et Belles-Lettres

Introduction

After more than thirty years of excavations in Nubia, the discovery in January 2003 of a cache of seven monumental stone statues constituted a wonderful moment for the University of Geneva's Archaeological Mission. These sculpted portraits of rulers from the late Twenty-fifth Dynasty and early Napatan Period are of major significance: on the one hand, they attest to the important role played by the Kerma region in the history of Nubian–Egyptian relations, on the other hand, they provide unprecedented information about the physical appearance of the depicted kings and, more generally, about stylistic developments in statuary of that period. Finally, the inscriptions to Amun of Pnubs, carved on the backs and bases of these statues confirm the identity of the main god and of the name given to the site after its conquest by Egyptian armies. It should be emphasized right away that this extraordinary discovery was just one aspect of the lengthy research into the origins of the history of the Sudan, which has been notably enriched in recent years thanks to the various surveys conducted in Middle and Upper Nubia. We now have a much better idea of the long-underestimated originality of Nubian culture and its deep roots in an extremely distant past. The weight of this Nubian tradition did not, however, rule out openness to other cultural models, particularly Egyptian.

Progressively penetrated by Egyptian monarchs in the course of military campaigns and expeditions, Nubia was a vast land traversed by the Nile, composed of regions stretching from the first to the fourth cataract and beyond. While the oldest evidences of Egyptian–Nubian contact is limited to Lower Nubia, by the Sixth Dynasty diplomatic, cultural, and economic relations between the Egyptian court at Memphis and the land of Yam had become customary. The difficulties encountered during the First Intermediate Period had made the Egyptians circumspect, inciting them to erect solid defenses on their borders, which they had moved several hundred kilometers farther south in order to thwart any new attempted invasions. The southern border of Egypt was then established at the second cataract, where a strong chain of fortresses was built, first to the north and then to the south of a vast zone of rapids that was called Batn al-Hagar ('Belly of the Rock'). This defensive system was efficient as long as the Egyptian government maintained firm control of it. But the weakness of the central government during the Second Intermediate Period allowed the kings of Kerma to win control of the area, at least until the first pharaohs of the Eighteenth Dynasty liberated Egypt from the Hyksos occupation and then reconquered the lost territories to the east and south.

The oldest evidence of a campaign conducted in Lower Nubia, from the end of the Second Intermediate Period, is some graffiti left at Toshka by soldiers of Kamose, the last king of the Seventeenth Dynasty. Following Kamose, Ahmose, the founder of the Eighteenth Dynasty, and his successor

View of the third cataract as seen
from the medieval fortress at Kagbar

Previous page:
Aerial view of the Nubian city of
Kerma with its temple precinct

Amenhotep I, confirmed their interest in the region by appointing an Egyptian official entrusted with significant powers. This "royal son of Kush," operated as a sort of viceroy who governed an entire civilian and military hierarchy. He was assisted by two deputies; one was responsible for Upper Nubia, the other for Lower Nubia. These men took back the old Egyptian fortresses, revamped them, and set up new fortified towns farther south. Thutmose I went one step further by personally leading his army to conquer the ancient kingdom of Kerma, which pushed the borders of Egypt south of the fourth cataract. The new border was thereafter marked by a rock near the Nile, locally known as Hagar al-Merwa, on which Thutmose I carved his cartouches. An account of the campaign that was inscribed on a rock at the third cataract, revealed the extent of the new Egyptian empire. The old kingdom of Kerma had not been perma-

nently vanquished, however, for further battles had to be won before the Egyptians would gain complete control over the area. Thutmose III finally confirmed Egyptian domination (which would last for centuries) when his cartouches were inscribed next to those of his predecessor on the rock of Hagar al-Merwa.

During the final decades of the Twentieth Dynasty, however, Lower Nubia was the scene of armed conflict between certain high-ranking officials and Upper Egyptian representatives of a pharaonic government that was increasingly restricted to the northern part of the country. Beginning with the Third Intermediate Period, the administrative division that arose between the traditional pharaohs and the High Priests of Amun—who also began assuming a monarchic role—seems to have further undermined the governance of an empire that was in fact becoming more

12

and more virtual (as illustrated by a fictionalized account of an Egyptian traveler to the Near East, written during that period and now known as *The Report of Wenamun.*) Egyptian remains in Nubia from that time are extremely rare. Thus the history of Sudan over the next three centuries remains fairly obscure to us—the few monuments that can be attributed with any certainty to that period are difficult to date with any precision. It was only toward the middle of the eighth century BCE that a princely family from the region of Napata, one of the largest sacred Kushite cities developed by the Egyptians, provided new epigraphic testimony written in Egyptian hieroglyphs.

Division between north and south was not the only division in Egypt, however; several distinct lineages struggled for power over a large part of the country. The former Libyan chieftains—who had been defeated and then integrated into the Egyptian population—took root and began fighting among themselves for control of the Delta region. One of them, Sheshonq, founded the Twenty-second Dynasty. Civil war erupted in Egypt, which was simultaneously enduring a threat from the Assyrian empire in the east. At that time a Kushite prince, Piankhy sought to pacify the Nile Valley even as he made himself the champion of traditional Egyptian values by harking back to the culture that the New Kingdom pharaohs had brought to Nubia six hundred years earlier. A monumental stela (now in the Egyptian Museum in Cairo) recounts the stages of Piankhy's victorious military campaign and successive re-establishment of Egyptian cults in one liberated city after another. For some one hundred years, all or part of Egyptian territory would thus fall under the hegemony of these rulers from Napata, who became known as the Twenty-fifth Dynasty. The 'Western Kingdom,' however—that is the Delta fief of the Libyan dynasts—effec-

Nubians bearing tribute.
Tomb of Huy, Tutankhamun's
viceroy of Kush

tively held out against Kushite armies even as Assyria once again threatened Egypt, eventually allying itself with the princes of Sais. The combination of these factors would lead to the defeat of Kushite forces.

Yet the century during which Egypt and Sudan were reunited under the authority of pharaohs from Upper Nubia would prove crucial for both countries. In Egypt, the Twenty-fifth Dynasty developed an original culture based on a return to the country's intellectual and artistic roots; in Sudan, this archaistic culture was consolidated, forging a local idiom that would thereafter serve as a key reference for Nubian monarchs once they were evicted from Egypt, following the reign of Tanutamun. His successor, Atlanersa, was the first in a Dynasty called Napatan, followed by the Meroitic Dynasty when, at some unknown date, the court retreated from Napata, downstream from the fourth cataract, to Meroe, upstream of the fifth cataract. In the second quarter of the fourth century BCE, Nastasen was the final monarch buried at Nuri, one of Napata's royal cemeteries. The Meroitic Dynasty can be traced down to the first quarter of the fourth century CE.

THE SITE

Kerma is located at the southern end of a vast alluvial plain upstream of the rapids of the third Nile cataract, on the right bank of the river. Khartoum, the capital of modern Sudan, is five hundred kilometers away; the border with Egypt is three hundred kilometers north (see map on page ii). In addition to its agricultural potential, the region offered the advantage of lying on a commercial crossroads linking Egypt to the Red Sea and to central Africa. It was certainly this particularly favorable location that led to the rise of the one of the oldest kingdoms on the African continent, beginning in the late third millennium BCE.

Previous page:
Aerial view of the Egyptian town of Doukki Gel

Right:
Topographic plan of the site of Kerma/Doukki Gel

1. Nubian town (Kerma)
2. Religious precinct, western Deffufa
3. Port zone; temple and royal tomb
4. Egyptian town (Doukki Gel)
5. Napatan neighborhood
6. Western necropolis

The Protohistoric Town

Human populations settled in the Kerma basin at a very early date, as witnessed by several Mesolithic and Neolithic sites. It should not be forgotten that until the end of the fourth millennium the climate there was still fairly humid. The presence of vegetation and multiple channels of the Nile would certainly have encouraged settlement by small communities, perhaps on a seasonal basis at first. In fact, the earliest traces of a human presence in the region—illustrated by a few rudimentary tools and animal bones that bear the marks of such cutting tools—date back some eight hundred thousand years. From 7500 BCE onward the remains become more significant: semi-buried dwellings, various objects and tools, and graves. These elements begin to provide some information about the lifestyles of populations that survived on river resources, hunting, and the gathering of grains. The Neolithic phase, from the late sixth to the fourth millennium BCE, is much better known and allows us to follow the stages of the spread of agriculture and the domestication of cattle in this period. Within certain groups, a hierarchy can be glimpsed through the organization of cemeteries and the composition of funerary artifacts. It is worth noting the often outstanding quality of grave furnishings, which included pottery, arrowheads, clubheads, harpoons, and items of finery. Residential areas can be reconstituted through post-holes that indicate the outlines of huts, enclosures, and fences, and by hearths, as well as a certain number of handmade objects and animal bones.

Around 3000 BCE a town grew up not far from the Neolithic dwelling place. Today some fifty circular huts have been identified, with an average diameter of four meters; in addition, there were two rectangular buildings whose function was probably special, and over three hundred pits designed to store food. The presence of large enclosures, testifying to the growing importance of livestock, and of stockades and a major system of defense, all complicate interpretation of the thousands of post-holes that have been unearthed. Here again, graves found in the immediate vicinity contained various and interesting furnishings. This town already seems to have belonged to a centrally governed chieftaincy, which would weigh upon the emergence of an independent kingdom at Kerma several centuries later.

Storage pits in
pre-Kerma settlement

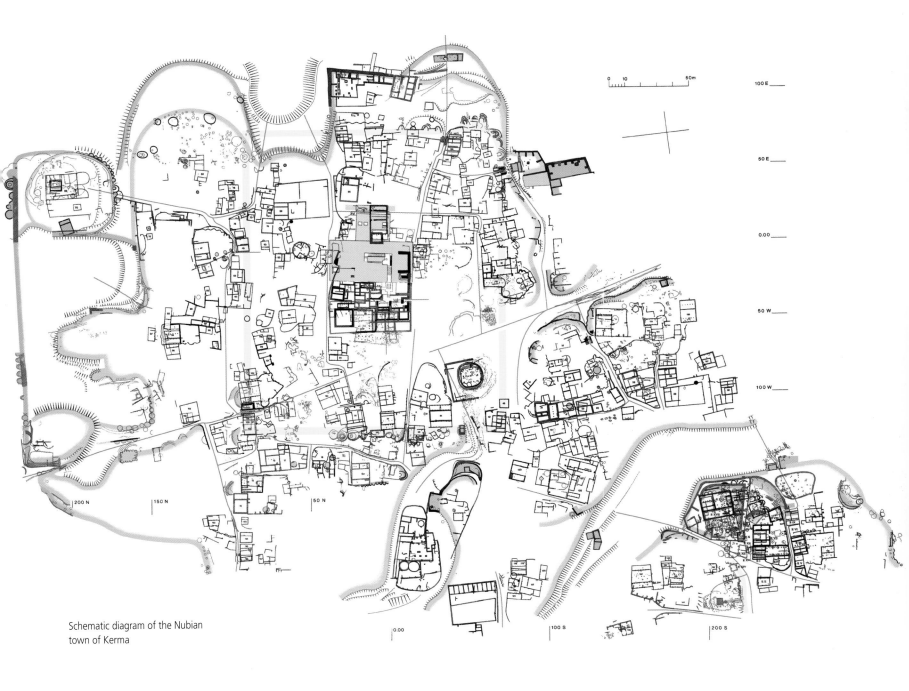

0   10   50m   100 E

50 E

0.00

50 W

100 W

200 N   150 N   50 N   0.00   100 S   200 S

Schematic diagram of the Nubian
town of Kerma

The Nubian Town and Its Necropolis

The town that succeeded the original village sometime around 2400 BCE was located roughly four kilometers to the west. This shift in the residential zone, observed elsewhere on the alluvial plain, was certainly due to changes in the hydrographic situation when certain channels of the Nile dried up. It is also worth noting that residents of the new town were buried in an enormous necropolis partly situated on the remains of the pre-Kerma settlement. Seals discovered in the oldest part of the cemetery indicate relations with lands close to the Red Sea. Further-

more, it is probable that a westward route, the famous Darb al-Arbain ('Forty-Day Trail'), was already being used in ancient times to transport herds of livestock. Thus, at a very early date the new kingdom had become a crossroads where numerous cultures came into contact. Even today, the various influences that have marked Nubia are apparent in the local architecture and the heterogeneity of its population.

In the past thirty years, systematic excavation of Nubian Kerma has presented a picture of a capital city in the third and

second millennia BCE. It is an exceptional find because vestiges of this kind are usually destroyed or buried under modern cities. Thus, it has been possible to locate several institutional precincts, such as the religious sector with its main temple and chapels designed as a place to worship deceased rulers; other impressive complexes represent royal residences and systems of defense built from earth or stone. The evolution of the residential area is highly complex, yet it is possible to identify social differences and a marked hierarchy. Furthermore, we might specu-

The Deffufa, or main temple
of Kerma

late about the general nature of this town, which seems to correspond above all to a protected zone reserved for an elite population. Whereas elsewhere in the kingdom we find towns that centralized agricultural products and villages that were situated alongside fields of crops, here in the capital we find spacious homes inhabited by dignitaries who monitored the trade in merchandise arriving from far-off lands, and who supervised shipments dispatched from administrative buildings.

Excavations around the Deffufa, the last of the original religious edifices built in the center of town, have shown how urban development took various construction techniques and materials into account. In Old Kerma (2450–2050 BCE),

religious buildings and special workshops for preparing offerings were built using the trunks of acacia trees, and roofed with palm fibers. These plant-based materials, once encased in hardened clay, could be painted in lively colors. The round huts were usually made of wood and clay. This method of construction, inspired by traditions dating back to prehistory, is still being used today. But only the most modest populations would perpetuate this practice. In religious buildings, we can distinguish strata of multiple reconstructions of one or another of the chapels; the post-holes that define the elevation of the walls often vary in diameter. The middle was reserved as a holy spot, sometimes emphasized by a hearth.

The mud-brick foundations
of houses

Around 2200–2000 BCE, the builders began using unfired mud-bricks. They would copy earlier buildings in this new material, retaining the unusual proportions of long, narrow constructions previously made of small beams (due to the lack of sufficiently tall trees). Builders also sought to consolidate the strong bases required by earthen architecture, which led to the appearance of massive abutments of brick used for fortifications. Later, the use of fired bricks constituted a significant change, because such material remained almost unknown elsewhere along the Nile Valley until the Late Period. Fired bricks were used as a facing to strengthen the base of town walls and also as structural material for a chapel built

with great care. The Classic Kerma Period (1750–1450 BCE), meanwhile, was characterized by the use of stone blocks that were more or less dressed. Here again, stones were used to reinforce defensive walls and structures, but could also be found in religious buildings and official storehouses.

The evolution suggested by structural details can also be observed in the layout of the town and its walls. The early settlement occupied an island whose alluvial terrace was defined by successive flooding, which lent great irregularity to the urban topography. The early ground plans nevertheless appear to obey a rectangular logic. It is probable that strong bastions protected the gates of a thick wall that enclosed a rather limited area. By the early Middle Kerma Period (2050–1750 BCE), bastioned fortifications already restricted the town to a surface of approximately one hundred by two hundred meters. The layout of the town was defined by these limits, and featured streets that followed an almost rectilinear pattern linking numerous gates. The religious precinct in the middle also followed the general rectilinear plan. A similar layout, on a smaller scale, is evident in a secondary settlement to the southwest, where several funerary chapels and workshops have been examined.

During the kingdom's heyday, Classic Kerma's need for space encouraged inhabitants to build outside the walls, along the access roads. All land on the alluvial plain was put to use, taking no account of the general layout of the town. More or less independent extensions thus sprang up even as the main protected routes were maintained: the heart of town was approached from low-lying roads that could be monitored from the bastions, and people then climbed toward the town gates between wooden stockades that helped to channel access. Rectangular and semi-circular bastions provided numerous points of defense, while buttressed walls seem to indicate a good knowledge of the large Egyptian fortresses on the second cataract, which clearly served as inspiration for Nubian builders.

The fortified settlement and its mortuary chapels

21

Kerma's geographic location—on the edge of the Egyptian empire and in contact with populations from central Africa and the Red Sea shoreline—makes it possible to postulate the existence of a network of exchanges with other lands, as substantiated by the discovery of various archaeological finds. In particular, the Nubian kings' audience chamber, rebuilt at least ten times on the same spot, bears no similarity to any Egyptian building; on the contrary, this chamber might be seen as a prototype for the large princely and royal huts attested on the African continent during the past four hundred years. Hence, there exists a link between the very ancient architecture of Kerma and buildings executed several millennia later. Such buildings offer an opportunity to rediscover the roots of an African architecture whose quality was so often mentioned by the earliest explorers and ethnologists. This comment in no way diminishes the originality of Nubian accomplishments, of which Kerma is a good example. The proximity of the Nile favored better protection and incited residents to dig deep ditches around the successive fortifications. The establishment of independent precincts, defined by winding or curving walls, proves that inhabitants sought to divide the town into special quarters with respective functions. Monumental gates suggest the existence of checkpoints even inside the urbanized zone.

One kilometer to the south of town there have emerged the vestiges of a settlement that might belong to a port district. Round buildings of wood date it to Middle Kerma occupation. The strata associated with these huts, washed by the passing waters, confirm the nearness of the river. During the Classic Kerma Period, a vast administrative building must have served to protect valuable merchandise, because it boasted stone walls that were

two meters thick. Furthermore, seal impressions with the names of Hyksos kings prove the existence of trade with Egypt's eastern Delta. Reserves of seal-making clay also indicate that Nubian products must have been exported. A temple and nearby chapel testify to religious worship that seems to have continued to the end of the kingdom's history. Indeed, the plan of the main temple is identical to those from the beginning of Egypt's New Kingdom, particularly the temple of Horus built at Buhen during the reign of Hatshepsut.

To grasp the interest and originality of Nubian peoples this quick archaeological survey must include a brief discussion of the enormous necropolis and the various funerary customs that were practiced at the time. Tumuli of at least twenty thousand graves extend over an area of 1,500 by 800 meters. The American archaeologist George Reisner, who excavated Kerma's western Deffufa, also dug up several thousand graves during three short seasons there, from 1913 to 1916. His observations provided a wealth of information, but Reisner's proposed chronology of the vestiges was backwards—he thought the most recent burials were the oldest. His work nevertheless remains highly useful, thanks to his meticulous description and classification of objects uncovered. The subsequent excavation of 350 additional tombs, yielded by twenty-seven test digs relatively distant from one another, has not revealed as many archaeological items but has made it possible to follow the main phases of Kerma cultures more precisely.

Old Kerma's earliest graves can be dated between 2500 and 2450 BCE. The graves are fairly deep and are marked on the surface by a circular superstructure made of small pieces of black stone placed in concentric circles. The tumulus was consoli-

dated by a one-meter ring of damp clay when the grave was built, white quartz pebbles were added, which gave greater consistency to the mound and minimized wind erosion. A second type of superstructure was built from small sandstone stelae some thirty to forty centimeters high, placed in a circle around the filled gravesite. The graves were very narrow and often oval shaped. The deceased was laid in a curled position on the leather blanket that he or she had used as bedding. Some corpses were covered with a second ox skin. Only modest furnishings were added, comprised of a very few pottery vessels and the occasional items of finery. At a very early date, some individuals were buried with a bow and arrows, and were sometimes accompanied by a dog.

Even in this early period, a shelter was sometimes erected to the northwest of certain tombs. Its light roof was placed on four posts, charred at their bases; the structure probably served as a funerary chapel. During burial ceremonies, meals were organized to the east of the grave, which remained open for a certain time. Overturned bowls on the ground indicated that food and drink had been shared with the deceased. Although graves were not initially differentiated by the wealth of furnishings or the size of the tumulus, within one or two centuries highly distinct graves began to appear. A hierarchy emerged among classes. Tombs became larger and adopted a circular plan. Whole sheep were interred alongside the deceased, and various vessels attest to the inclusion of products required in everyday life. A bit later, the practice arose of depositing bucrania, or ox skulls—the remains of banquets prepared in town—to the south of the tumulus.

Mud bricks were used in the necropolis, as they were in town, and several small funerary structures were built of brick dur-

The often rebuilt
audience chamber

ing the Middle Kerma Period. Of modest
dimensions—one meter by two—they
were always placed on the northwest side
of the tumulus. Solid stakes were driven
into the ground to the north to hold a
windscreen, which was needed to protect
the ceremony from potentially strong gusts
of wind. Overturned bowls on the eastern
edge of the grave showed that a meal continued to be shared with the deceased.
Deposits of bucrania to the south grew significantly. For a single princely tomb—
some two meters deep and twelve meters
in diameter, below a tumulus that mea-

sured thirty to forty meters in diameter—
there were no fewer than 4,500 ox skulls.
All the animals in the herd were thus
included, and even if collective banquets
took place over a period of months while
the bucrania were subsequently deposited
at once, the extraordinary investment in
the funeral rites for a single individual can
hardly be ignored.

The organization of graves remained
unchanged over a period of centuries. The
deceased was always placed in a curled or
bent position on the right side, with his or
her arms folded in front of the face, and

1200 N
1100 N
1000 N
900 N
800 N
700 N
600 N
500 N
400 N
300 N
200 N
100 N
00.0
100 S
200 S
300 S

0   100m

4
3
1
27
2   5
6   23
N
22
21
8   7
20
9
10   25   11
12
14
13   24
M
15
16
19
17
18
XI
II

Old Kerma
Old/Middle Kerma
Middle Kerma
Classic Kerma

400 W   300 W   200 W   100 W   00.0   100 E   200 E   300 E   400 E

Topographic diagram
of the eastern necropolis
with color-coded dating

always turned north. The head, at the east end, might rest on a cushion of organic material. Gradually, the leather blankets were replaced by beds made of wood and leather straps. The beds were decorated with feet carved in the form of animal hooves, and inlaid with bronze or ivory. On the north side, furnishings included a great number of vessels as well as small stands on which they were placed. All kinds of food and cosmetics deemed to be useful in a future life, have been identified: grains, milk products, bread, resin, perfumes, and so on; carefully sliced pieces of mutton were also habitually included. Human sacrifices, already practiced during earlier periods, also became more numerous in this period. The age and sex of the individuals sacrificed suggest that certain members of the family had to follow the deceased into the afterlife. Whole goats and sheep were perhaps part of another ritual, because the heads of some sheep still bear a disk of ostrich features affixed to a leather holder. This find easily conjures an image of the god Amun in his ram-headed form, attested at a much later date.

The last graves dug at the necropolis are of exceptional size; some tumuli are nearly one hundred meters in diameter. The graves themselves progressively took on a rectangular shape. The wealth of funerary objects encouraged grave robbers to profane the tombs; the significant number of gold items inevitably aroused the covetousness of treasure hunters. Extant vestiges nevertheless illustrate the extraordinary development of Classic Kerma culture. Kings asserted their power by planning their own funerary cult and by having hundreds of people sacrificed at the time of their death. Northwest of certain tumuli there are vague traces of chapels with painted decoration, though more information is provided by partially preserved paintings in the two temples.

Tumulus over an Old
Kerma grave

A Middle Kerma grave

There, on the walls representing Egyptian territory, we can see familiar Egyptian scenes of fishing, bullfighting, and boating. In contrast, on the walls depicting Nubian lands are covered with an African menagerie including hippopotami, oxen, and especially giraffes.

Nearly one thousand years of uninterrupted cultural development came to an end with the first military campaigns by Egyptian pharaohs of the early Eighteenth Dynasty. These upheavals led to the abandonment of the cemetery, which was moved closer to town and into the port district. There, a royal tomb was built in the form of a large circle of stepped stones six meters deep. The funeral chamber could be reached by a monumental staircase that was subsequently covered by a chapel. A vast tumulus, edged by a mudbrick wall faced with fired bricks, rose above the central part. This unusual type of grave belonged to an important individual and was filled with rich furnishings. It was willfully destroyed at some point, when all the material placed in the tomb was hacked to pieces. Shortly afterward, the city itself was abandoned by the native population.

The paving in temple K II, composed of reused stelae

The Egyptian Town

One kilometer north of the Nubian capital, a new city was founded by the pharaohs of the early Eighteenth Dynasty. The fortified town was built on a site now characterized by tall red mounds of broken molds for making bread that was used for temple offerings. This settlement is therefore known by the Nubian term Doukki Gel, which can be translated as 'red mound.' Roughly one hundred years ago George Reisner made the first exploratory search here but did not come up with any conclusive material. We ourselves waited twenty years before undertaking any work there as it required the extension of a road—to the detriment of vestiges—in order for a salvage program to be drawn up in conjunction with Sudan's director of excavations, Salah Eldin Mohamed Ahmed. However, we persevered because we deemed the exploration

of Doukki Gel crucial to our understanding of the transition between the end of the powerful Kerma kingdom and the early stages of Egyptian colonization. Furthermore, fragments of inscriptions found on the surface suggested that certain later texts might provide historical information of great interest.

The Doukki Gel site suffered greatly from the planting of crops that followed an English irrigation project in the 1920s. The entire area between the two ancient towns is currently flooded, though a few partial discoveries have brought to light graves from a necropolis that dates from the Meroitic Period (between 400 BCE and 400 CE). A few rich funerary chambers have yielded remarkable material that indicates the quality of the pottery and bronze workshops during that period. We

erected a wall around the archaeological site to protect the nearby mounds and land that formed terraces, but several houses and a large palm grove still occupy a significant part of the Egyptian town. Despite all these constraints, the excavation of a temple and palace precinct finally began ten years ago. It was decided that the highest mound, close to the ancient bakeries, would be conserved since it typifies this field of ruins and continues to remind us of the religious function of the settlement.

It should be immediately pointed out that the manner in which the archaeological strata and the walls are superposed constitutes a highly complex series of layers; over a two-thousand-year period people repeatedly demolished and rebuilt religious edifices and their outbuildings. Analysis

Aerial photograph
of the Egyptian town
of Doukki Gel

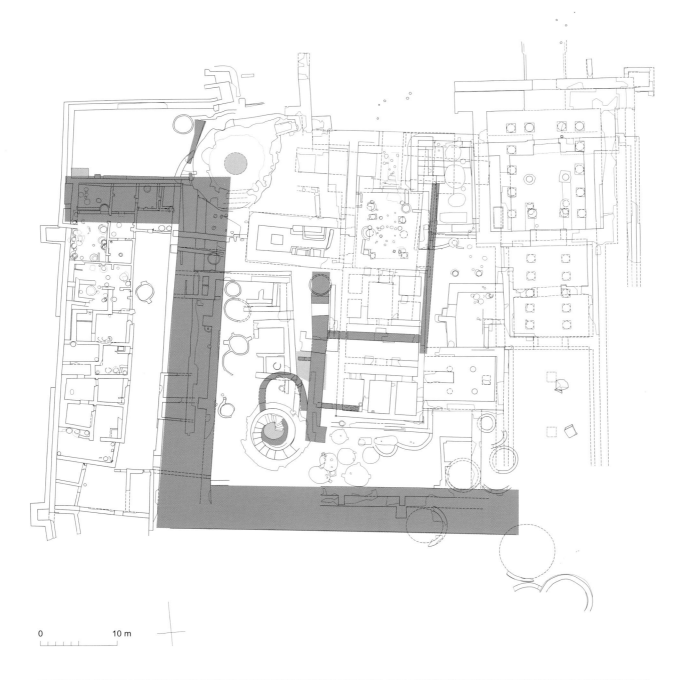

Schematic diagram of the vestiges of Doukki Gel from the reign of Thutmose III

0   10 m

Segment of a buttressed wall in the Egyptian town

28

Fragment of a cartouche
of Thutmose III

must therefore be carried out in such a way that each transformation can be progressively distinguished. In the current state of excavation, two wells have attracted particular attention: some thirty meters apart, they might have originally dictated the organization of this precinct and of the buildings erected to the southwest. The wells have undergone numerous modifications, but during the early phases of habitation they were accessed by rather unusual means. The well to the north, for instance, had an impressive ceremonial staircase that was built with roughly hewn stones. Such structures made from raw blocks of various sorts recall a mode of construction employed late in the Classic Kerma Period, as seen in a wide-mouthed well at the grave of one of the last local monarchs. Moreover, fragments found near the staircase correspond to materials used at the end of the Kerma Period, mixed with typically Egyptian ceramics. The position of the staircase and its location suggest that this often-restored feature was perhaps originally designed as a sacred lake, which became a multi-purpose well a thousand years later.

The second well was given a circular facing of sandstone blocks that have been eroded by the water. This structure visibly descends to a great depth, below a well entirely reconstructed during the Meroitic Period. Laterally, however, an underground passage seems to have been dug during an early period of use. One or two steps suggest that people descended a curved passage to reach the water table. Access must have begun in a room next to the original temple. Here again, archaeological material found on the spot seems to indicate a transitional period, because Classic Kerma pottery is mixed with shards of Egyptian turned pottery from the early Eighteenth Dynasty.

The surviving fragments of a wall identify the city as Egyptian. Masonry six meters thick is composed of parallel, back-to-back walls, belonging to various states of fortification. Clearing the mud bricks brought to light buttresses or niched walls typical of a system adopted by the Egyptians for fortified towns in border lands or occupied territory. The powerful walls of Doukki Gel were appropriate to a major center potentially threatened by uprisings of the local population or attacks from enemy peoples. Similar cities usually display a rectangular plan. It is therefore surprising to note that the wall stops and turns at the level of the northern well or 'sacred lake,' thus forming a salient to the west (see diagram on page 28). This layout is hard to explain; the enormous wall will have to be followed in order to discover the reasons for the change in direction.

Alongside and underneath vestiges of later temples there emerged foundations some two meters thick that belong to the lateral, mud-brick walls of a major religious edifice. A western gate has been located; it was built of stone, but almost nothing remains in place. Its sandstone blocks, with high-quality decoration, were found in fragments where the gate stood. One of those fragments features part of a cartouche with the name of Thutmose III. Other segments of wall indicate that the building was at least fifteen meters wide. At its southern end, test digs have shown that a workshop with furnaces must have extended beyond the sanctuary. Indeed, a great number of *tuyères*, or ceramic blow tubes, were laid there with care; several of which were in relatively good condition. Flat, round bread molds can potentially be linked to the use of these tuyères even though such tubes were more often used for hydraulic installations or for smelting metal. However, no trace of bronze has been found. Once again, Classic Kerma pottery and Egyptian shards were found in the same context.

Having described the early phases of this Egyptian settlement, we can see that the founding of the town represented a break with the Nubian capital, even if new religious buildings on the new site replaced various religious establishments already located there. Of course, our research is not complete, and if we take into account fortified Egyptian towns explored farther north, it appears that the site excavated at

Doukki Gel corresponds only to the precinct reserved for religious edifices, which are usually clustered with their out-buildings along one side of a town. Thus we lack the storehouse quarter where food-stuffs and items of tribute the local population had to deliver to the Egyptian viceroy would be stocked. Nor have we located the dwellings of military and civil-ian authorities, nor the houses occupied by other Egyptians or indeed by certain Nubians. However, it might be useful to complement these topographic observa-tions with a description of sectors that have been partially excavated, where sev-eral contemporaneous or posterior clues contribute to a picture of the religious precinct and the town.

It was probably during the reigns of Thutmose IV and Akhenaten that this New

Kingdom architectural ensemble assumed its full scope. The large mud-brick edifice was transformed, and a temple was founded by Thutmose IV on the same spot, follow-ing a similar layout. The temple pylon was erected next to the well or sacred lake to the north, while the southern well was very close to the sanctuary. Outbuildings extended westward. A private cult practiced there, one whose roots were probably more ancient. Grain storage pits were built in this precinct and also to the south, behind the enclosed sanctuary. Constructed in an irreg-ular fashion, the storage silos were consolidated with stones and hardened clay in order to sustain the weight of the grain. Nearby, rounded courtyards were probably allocated to the artisans who made the bread used in offerings. Other outbuildings complete the installations against the wall.

The existence of a second New Kingdom temple has been confirmed on the east side. It was rebuilt several times and its original plan remains almost totally unknown. The only elements that cur-rently point to a reconstitution are the lower courses of the lateral walls, two bases of columns for a portico courtyard, and a floor found beneath later levels of occupation. It should be noted that the orientation of the edifice differs slightly from the neighboring temple, but the two pylons must have been side by side. The respective axes of the two buildings met to the north where there perhaps existed a quay at the end of a dromos whose traces have not yet been found. This unconven-tional north-south orientation might be explained by the meanderings of the Nile, since religious buildings were often laid out perpendicular to the river bed—notably when it was close by—rather than according to the points of compass. Now, it seems probable that the Egyptian town, like the Nubian capital, arose on an island. The orientation of the Kerma culture's religious buildings may also have played a role, because all of these sacred buildings are placed on a north-south axis, the only difference being that their doors tended to open onto the south side.

Along the path defined by the extension of the axis of the Doukki Gel temples, a strange, later building provides some additional information on the town. It is a Meroitic edifice that incorporated older construction materials; we were obliged to carry out an emergency excavation since local quarrying of sand threatened this zone. Against all expectations, a square building some sixteen meters per side emerged; its outer walls, two meters thick, were excavated. It has not been possible, however, to identify the various states or internal structures. Yet given its distance from the temple facades—over three hundred meters—this building provides a yardstick for assessing the boundaries of the fortified town, which in this case appears to have been vast. If this hypothesis is confirmed, the road leading from the religious precinct would have passed right next to this unearthed structure and would have ended in the banks of sand that perhaps correspond to one of the dried-up channels of the river.

In front of the two temple pylons there emerged, at a certain depth, the vestiges of a paved lane of great quality, made of abutting flagstones and worn by frequent use. The path of this lane is not perfectly rectilinear, for it veers slightly to the west. In an initial configuration, the lane must have turned back toward the eastern temple; the placing and color of the sandstone slabs are proof that this original layout existed in

The paved way
leading to the New
Kingdom palace

Far left:
The stairs leading to the sacred lake

two states. Later, the lane would have been cut, and then extended in the direction of the gate of the second temple, twenty meters farther west. In front of that gate, two successive levels of paving can be seen, sloping slightly near the buildings. The way must have been flanked by low walls, as has been noted elsewhere, and a processional halting station might have been added later, since post-holes were drilled into the slabs at some point. They might be the traces left by a ceremonial canopy. On both sides of the road, considerable quantities of New Kingdom potshards were found.

Fifty to seventy meters from the temple entrances, at the opposite end of this lane, the meager remains of a ceremonial palace have also been unearthed. The palace was composed of several rooms made of mud brick. Although part of the premises have vanished from erosion, it is still possible to observe—despite later restorations—the outline of the main block of two rooms flanked on each side by several annexes. A small, hidden door to the southwest facilitated access. In front of the central rooms a massive stone structure left the negative imprint of its foundation blocks; they sketch the outlines of a monumental gate, inside which the paved lane continued at a slight slope. The quality of this complex and the determination to maintain it to the end of the Meroitic Period suggests that it was associated with royal ceremonial processions.

Sand removal on the south side of the palace revealed Nile deposits that immediately predate the building of the palace. Imagine our surprise in discovering the surface of a field worked with a plow: the furrows and overturned clumps had remained frozen in time, for over three millennia. On the edge of the field we could make out the well-preserved hoofprints of the oxen that drew the plow. It was clear how the animals turned at the end of one row to head down the next furrow. The many potshards date this plowing work to the Classic Kerma Period. The extent of the field not yet having been measured, this discovery raises a fundamental problem: although the earth had clearly been damp during plowing, it had never been sown with seed—the plowed field was simply left as it was. Hence it is hard not to wonder whether we are dealing here with the tangible traces of some foundation ritual.

Farther south in the same sector, other excavations are planned. A few building blocks of gray sandstone arranged as though for foundations might be contemporary with the New Kingdom buildings. The structure is in a wretched state of preservation, but it might be part of the sacred complex. Returning to the two temples, unambiguously located in the center-west of the precinct, it is worth mentioning various secondary structures that must have created, in stages, a transitional zone between the two. Thus a room or courtyard was laid out behind the piers of the two pylons. It could be entered from a colonnaded courtyard immediately to the south, which linked the two buildings. Farther south still, a bronze-making workshop is identifiable from round furnaces with a bellows system used to smelt small objects. The workshop functioned for centuries. A Twenty-fifth Dynasty chapel set up near the temples might have older origins, to judge by its similar arrangement to a transversal chapel next to the main temple B 500 at Gebel Barkal, which has been attributed to Ramesses II.

The temple outbuildings assumed considerable scope throughout the history of the site, and it might be supposed that already in the Eighteenth and Nineteenth Dynasties the special precinct extended to the south. The storage silos were included in it. Yet farther east there laid rubbish deposits, one to two meters deep, in which large quantities of shards of bread molds were dumped. These cylindrical molds were very smooth and regular inside, and are characteristic of that period.

The topography of the Egyptian town should yield many other remains, judging by the accumulation of rubble and the depth of layers above the level of the second millennium BCE. Such discoveries will nevertheless depend on the preservation of those deep layers where mud bricks are often hard to distinguish.

A field plowed prior to construction of the New Kingdom building

Kerma after the Egyptians

The site of Doukki Gel certainly enjoyed a boom period during the Twenty-fifth Dynasty. It was part of the vast Kushite kingdom whose capital, Napata, developed near the sacred mountain of Gebel Barkal, a religious complex some two hundred kilometers farther up the Nile, where the waters were calm and where crop fields lined the river. The kingdom also extended to territories that ran much farther south, vaulting the granite barriers of the fourth to sixth cataracts. To the north of Kerma, meanwhile, beyond the arid lands that dominated the region between the third and first cataracts, it was all of Egypt that ultimately came under the control of the powerful Kushite kings, "Lords of the Two Lands." Despite the exceptional

nature of this period, which lasted roughly a century, almost no contemporaneous buildings survive at Kerma, even though it is clear that an impressive renaissance occurred everywhere.

Nevertheless, we can be certain that the sacred precinct at Doukki Gel was restored during the reign of the Kushite kings. The proof lies in the large stone blocks decorated with bas-reliefs of pharaoh Shabaqo, reused in a bench placed in front of the eastern temple. Major reconstruction in mud brick was done behind the pylons, between the entrance courtyards to the two temples. The architectural concept of a transversal chapel erected alongside the temple sanctuaries is entirely comparable to other buildings of the reign of Taharqa.

It should not be forgotten that it was in the days of Taharqa that a series of remarkable temples was built at Sanam, Kawa, and Tabo. This latter site, twelve miles south of Kerma, offers a glimpse of construction methods that demonstrate a return to Egyptian sources. The extremely classical layout of the temple, repeated in all three towns, imitated an earlier model probably originating from Memphis. The iconographical subjects are part of a tradition that marks the phases of a veritable Egyptianization of Nubia.

Burial practices offer insight into Egyptian influences on a local milieu where the old rites of the Kerma culture were nevertheless not forgotten. Indeed, in the southwest part of the Nubian city,

Cartouche of King Shabaqo,
Twenty-fifth Dynasty

Right:
Kushite grave in the
Nubian tradition

tombs from the New Kingdom followed by those of the Twenty-fifth Dynasty feature burial in a curled position, with relatively abundant grave furnishings. The rectangular graves were covered by a superstructure of mud bricks. Other tombs in the same cemetery, however, are completely different even though the few surviving deposits show that the pottery was of the same period. Such tombs are composed of a steep corridor leading to a chamber dug from the alluvial substrate or partially constructed with a vault of mud brick. Here the deceased were stretched out on their backs and placed in a sarcophagus of wood or pasteboard, sometimes plastered and painted.

This second style of burial ultimately superseded the older customs. Furthermore, the imagery on the sarcophagi belongs to the standard repertoire found in Egypt: multi-strand necklaces incorporating the open-winged motif and funerary deities including Thoth—in his ibis form—and Anubis. It is also worth noting that beaded nets were placed on the bodies of deceased females. Although no objects were found next to the deceased, the steep corridors contained goblets used for libations. It is probable that these tombs were topped by a mud-brick pyramid, like the stone pyramids of the grand Kushite kings buried near the capital. Also at Napata were many graves in which the body was still arranged in a curled position, but then there was a progressive move away from this popular tradition in favor of the new Egyptian custom.

Residential areas had to move outside the fortified town, at least partially. To the southwest of Doukki Gel, in the direction of the Nile, a large, square residential building has been uncovered. A second residence of the same type was located nearby. It can be assumed that the settlement was already fairly vast in Taharqa's

The foundations of a Napatan residential building in the modern town

reign, and during subsequent periods the buildings were further enlarged and a pottery workshop began producing large quantities of Napatan ceramics. The large residence was renovated and transformed at least four times. It had storehouses on the ground floor and an upper floor where living spaces were accessible by stairs or ramps. Also uncovered in the pottery workshop were the remains of a small quadrangular house of mud brick and pits for preparing and soaking the clay. Later, the house was replaced by circular huts.

Such reconstructions, which are well-attested in this somewhat removed settlement, demonstrate continuous activity during the late Twenty-fifth Dynasty and into the founding of the Napatan and Meroitic empires. Such continuity is confirmed at Doukki Gel and its necropolises, where architectural structures in the religious precinct and the extension of burial zones to the site of the former Nubian city provide so many indications of it. The cache of royal statues is a key element in dealing with this historical evolution and the revival of Nubia, which continued to

Faience vessel from a Kushite tomb

36

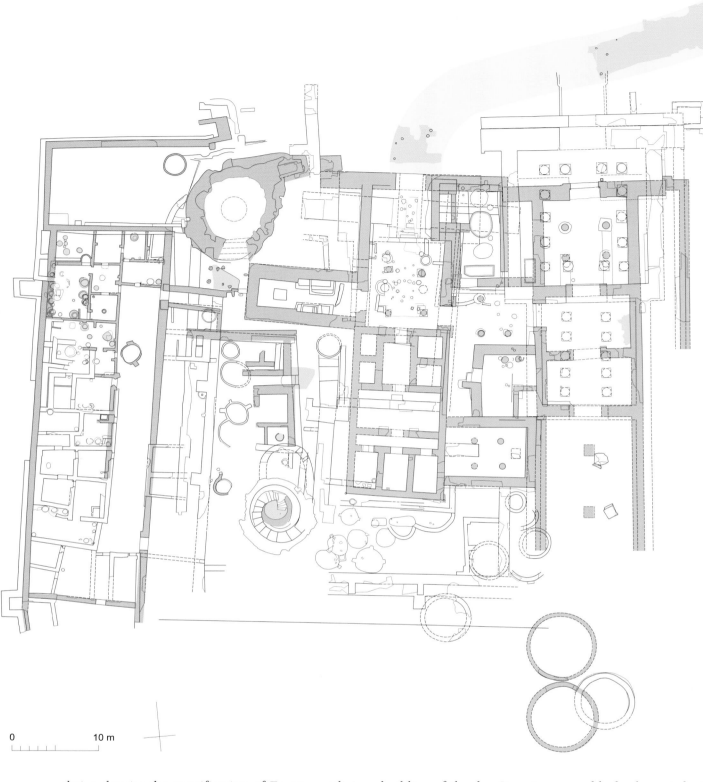

0   10 m

thrive despite the reunification of Egypt under the Psamtiks. It was henceforth an independent country that would exist for a millennium in Kush, once again developing an original civilization. Even though Egyptian influences were incontrovertible, this regional power was also linked to central Africa.

The temples at Doukki Gel were almost completely rebuilt, perhaps at the initiative of Irike-Amanote, whose throne name, Neferibre, was discovered on two blocks abandoned during exploitation of the site at the end of the Meroitic era. The remains of the eastern temple give an idea of a large religious building of the day. Its entrance has survived to a height of roughly one meter. The frame of the door and the threshold are of stone, whereas the pylon was built of mud brick, as were the side walls. The columns of the colonnaded first court were re-used from the earlier temple. A second door, in line with the first, gave onto a room whose floor was paved with reused blocks taken from the temple of Aten. Although the vestibule and the other rooms of the temple have been destroyed, we can see in their place two enormous monolithic blocks that served as the base of a naos, statue, or sacred barque. These blocks decorated with moldings help us to reconstitute the missing architectural features (see diagram above).

The neighboring temple was also restored with a narrow but lengthened pylon. Later Meroitic modifications, however, make it hard to interpret the masonry. During the Napatan Period, the space between the entrance courts of the two temples was occupied by an L-shaped room, flanked on its eastern side by a long courtyard or outbuilding. Several internal features, including the cache, testify to the importance of this room, which would long remain a holy

place. On the other side of the temple, to the west, a chapel perpendicular to the main axis ran toward the northern well. The well was steadily modified and a large ceremonial court created an open space on its western edge. An entrance from the court probably existed, but another structure also rose to the north.

From the Twenty-fifth Dynasty, attempts must have been made to extend the western zone that serviced the temples. The bakeries and butcher shops created rubbish that invaded the surrounding area, since dumps formed along the outer wall, which would soon be leveled in order to incorporate the vast outbuildings into the temple complex. A startling overall unit was then developed. It occupied a surface forty-five meters long by fifteen to twenty meters wide. Bordering a long courtyard, a series of production workshops supplied bread, meat, and probably beer to the western temple. Each shop opened onto an inner courtyard where there stood batteries of circular ovens and underground or above-ground silos, demonstrating the productivity required for everyday needs. In a smaller space, a deep layer of young oxen bones represents the remains of butchered meat.

Access to the two wells, which also served as a water supply, has been reconstructed through remnants of an independent corridor and special passageways. The foundation walls of a square structure represent part of a central building that must have coordinated the distribution of offerings sent into the temple via an aligned door. This extraordinary architectural complex, comparable to the outbuildings of the Ramesseum in Egypt, continued all around both temples: mounds of fragments of bread molds indicate the general layout of these annexes. Our excavations have therefore uncovered

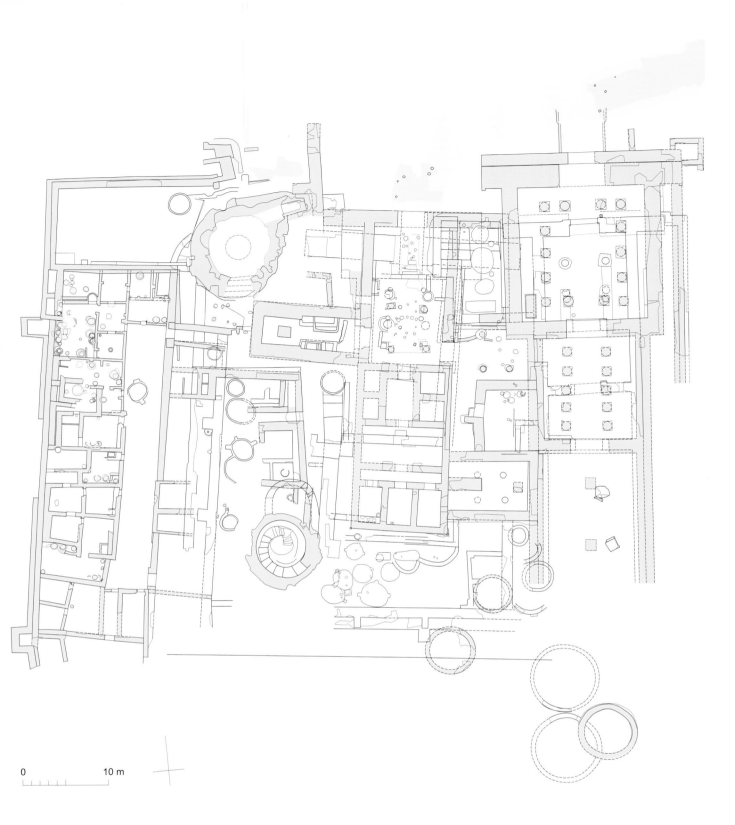

0   10 m

only one part of these outbuildings, whose southern and eastern sectors probably produced even greater quantities of offerings, because the heaps of potshards and ash rise over eight meters high. In all such sectors of the site, round silos demonstrate that these activities called for considerable reserves of grain.

The Napatan necropolis must have primarily occupied a site to the north of the former Nubian city. We have observed traces of hundreds of very long, narrow ditches indicating descent shafts to funerary chambers buried deep below ground.

Sometimes there survives a basin-shaped offering table made of sandstone, coarsely carved with images of food and vases. Since the land has been severely eroded, all traces of superstructures have vanished. Yet comparison with a contemporaneous cemetery in Tabo suggests that many graves were topped by brick pyramids. Given the length of the access stairways, a reconstitution of the pyramids would imply that they were over ten meters high. Burials in sarcophagi would continue to be practiced for a long time, and meticulous cleaning of the termite-

riddled wooden components generally reveals painted outlines.

The Meroitic Period reached its heyday during the reign of King Natakamani and Queen Amanitore, shortly before the start of the Christian era. Traces of all kinds are visible throughout the archaeological site of Kerma. The most impressive feature is probably the demographic growth, apparent from the increase in the number of tombs. These graves occupy cemeteries that cover not only the plots of the Nubian town but also large areas all around. Of course these tombs, which have not been systematically excavated, were progressively built over a period that spanned eight centuries, yet the quality of furnishings from the classic period remains outstanding. In large, underground chambers built from mud brick, with perfectly developed vaulting, and doors often modified to accommodate several series of burials—some tombs contain up to ten or twelve individuals—Kerma's craft workshops left objects of very high quality. Whether they made bronze bowls finely thinned on a lathe and then tin-plated, or astonishing painted pottery whose decorative diversity is remarkable, all these wares prove the presence of a social elite highly sensitive to artistry. The tombs also contained gold and silver finery, decorated with semi-precious stones, as well as faience amulets. Naturally, these graveyards were

robbed long ago, but the profusion of remains has meant that some significant vestiges have survived. A few brick foundation courses have made it possible to reconstruct, here and there, the base of pyramids that rose near the still imposing ruins of the Deffufa. The ancient monument must have inspired great respect, and even today people refer to the ghosts that live there.

The religious precinct of Doukki Gel was almost entirely rebuilt, taking into account earlier structures that guided the outlines of newer buildings (see diagram on page 40). The use of fired brick makes this general renovation highly perceptible, and it often happened that a facing of mud brick would be retained even while a more solid structure of fired brick covered the original masonry. Elsewhere, a doubling of the wall made it possible to allow worship to con-

tinue inside until the obsolete elements were later razed. This mixture of materials, to which the occasional use of blocks of stone should be added, is highly apparent in the walls of temples, although these buildings received a decoration of painted plaster that would have masked the diversity of materials. Grander proportions were thus given to the eastern temple, whose entrance was preceded by a very simple dromos bordered—at least at the surviving end—by low walls of mud brick.

This eastern temple is one of the largest Meroitic sanctuaries in Sudan, being nearly fifty-five meters long and boasting a pylon twenty-five meters wide. A few surviving fragments suggest that the façade must have been decorated with high-relief carvings of the king, larger than life, whose body was painted in red ocher. Elements of a frieze and hieroglyphic signs

Classic Meroitic pottery

with prophylactic function were found on other fragments of plaster collected at the foot of the façade. Once past the large gate that required a thickening of the pylon, one entered a peristyle court whose columns were set on square bases. A second door led to the hypostyle hall whose ten columns shared a single foundation. The earlier Napatan monolithic base,

described above, was salvaged and placed in line with the restored transversal chapel, in what must have been the center of a vestibule. The second base was perhaps placed in the aligned sanctuary, probably tripartite. A temenos separated the eastern side wall from the fortress wall, remains of which are detectable running eastward from the pylon.

The transversal chapel still seems to have been connected to this temple; it was heavily reworked and facings of fired brick were added to its stone wall. Certain sections of wall that had crumbled during periods of abandonment were redone. A staircase led to an altar at the back, against the far wall, made of mud brick. Against the chapel's north

wall, the bronze-smelting workshop was still active and was used to make little Meroitic objects. Statuettes of Osiris have come to light in significant quantities in the temple, and they certainly came—as did ram's heads crowned by a sun-disk and decorated pins—from the bronze-maker's kilns, beside which discarded molds have been found. Several round silos indicate that the New Kingdom wall had been demolished and that to the south there was thereafter direct access to the outbuildings.

The second temple also underwent complete transformation. The colonnaded court was extended northward. The sanctuary and its surroundings did not survive the upheavals that occurred after worship was halted and the building materials were scavenged. Strangely, the protruding chapel to the west of the courtyard survived best, despite dramatic fire damage. The construction method employed on this chapel was unusual. Known as *opus africanum,* it reused building blocks, which were stacked in vertical fashion, the gaps were filled with bricks. After the fire, the walls took on a more conventional appearance. Both states were contemporaneous with the Classic Meroitic Period. The reconstruction campaign also affected the ceremonial courtyard to the northwest as well as all the outbuildings. The walls were doubled and the various service workshops underwent major alterations related to a change in the level of the ground. The central distribution building was also rebuilt.

Serious work was carried out on the two wells. The southern well was topped by a raised structure made from an inner facing of fired brick with infill of mud brick. In magisterial fashion, the master mason decorated this raised portion with courses of horizontal bricks alternated with vertically set bricks. The effect is striking, as is the spiral staircase with impressive stone steps leading down to the New Kingdom well retained at the bottom. The northern well flared at the top into a wide ring of added clay. A stair on the south side provided access from the outbuildings, while the north side was built up into a kind of pool raised on three sides with reused blocks, sometimes decorated with bas-reliefs. The northern terrace was probably part of a ceremonial itinerary—an amazing bronze processional censer was found on this spot.

The New Kingdom palace to the east was no longer reached via a path of paved sandstone, which had by this time been covered by an accumulation of sand and earth. Major restoration was done on the palace throughout several periods; most apparent are the fired-brick facings done during the Meroitic era. Fifty meters to the north, a large rectangular edifice might also be interpreted as another, more residential, palace. It was built on land where some vestiges of Classic Kerma and Napatan structures exist. Despite the degraded condition of this building, we can nevertheless make out a reception hall or courtyard that was square in the center, surrounded by vaulted corridors. Two colonnaded rooms speak to the care paid to the interior architecture. In reconstituting the western part of this palace, we might suggest linking it to a potential dromos or path leading from the eastern temple to the massive buildings located near the other end of town, several hundred meters to the north.

During the fourth century CE the temples and dwellings were deserted, and a population with different traditions moved into the region. Two centuries later, Christianity arrived in turn, though only a few tombs testify to a new cycle of development at Kerma, followed by successive stages of Islamization. Christian settlements sprang up throughout the basin upstream of the third cataract, but the old archaeological sites seem to have been abandoned despite a growing population. After several millennia, the city of Kerma/Doukki Gel lost its eminence in spite of its favorable geographical location. The Christian capital of one of the three Sudanese kingdoms was founded farther south, at Old Dongola, where grandiose, superbly decorated churches constituted a new center of influence.

Ceremonial censer
of bronze

THE DISCOVERY

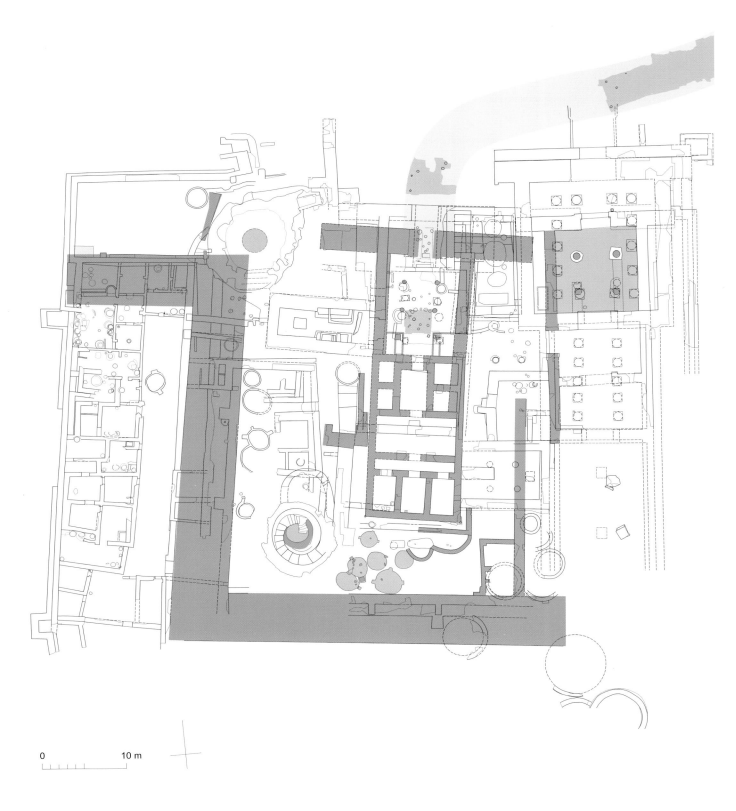

0   10 m

A Temple to Amun of Pnubs

It seems to have been the southwest corner of the city where the main works commissioned by the great pharaohs of the Eighteenth Dynasty were carried out. Successive phases of rebuilding on this site make analysis of the vestiges very complicated. The remains of various religious edifices are often limited to a few fragmentary mounds of mud brick, to the negative imprint of certain walls, or to a few blocks still in situ. Ongoing research will provide additional information to our knowledge of these temples, and comparison with well-preserved, contemporaneous buildings found elsewhere should make it possible to follow this period during which construction seems to have been almost continuous from one reign to another. Although we have seen how difficult it is to reconstitute the precise stages of the founding of the Egyptian city, it might be useful to go over the gradual development of a key religious edifice, the various states of which will help to explain the presence of a much later cache.

The work carried out by Thutmose III and his son Amenhotep II demonstrates that Nubia was enjoying a more peaceful period. Uprisings of the local population against the occupiers had quieted, and the building of temples was part of the reorganization of social and religious life. Although Thutmose IV had put down a rebellion in the eighth year of his reign, the Egyptian empire regained full authority along this part of the Nile Valley despite its great distance from the seat of royal power. The first Doukki Gel temple for which we can currently reconstruct a coherent picture was built during the reign of Thutmose IV. A direct descendent of Amenhotep II, Thutmose IV was another great builder despite his relatively brief reign of ten years. He often modified his predecessors' buildings in Egypt and Nubia with additions or alterations. At Doukki Gel these renovations were part of a more ambitious architectural project, even if some earlier structures were incorporated into the overall plan.

After we cleared away two or three meters of infill, the remaining vestiges began to appear, now in highly degraded form. *Sebbakhin*—those heavy consumers of archaeological earth (with which they enrich the soil in their fields)—had demolished the mud-brick walls even as builders salvaged the stones and fired bricks, which were valued as rare construction materials. The blocks were often cut up in the ditches prior to reuse. These strata of destruction that followed abandonment of the site are nevertheless crucial to our study, for many fragments bearing inscriptions or bas-relief decoration have turned up there. Thus hundreds of such carved stones now provide us with information on the way the buildings were restored and how they looked. Once all the rubble and fill was removed, it became possible to reveal original elements still in place, and to situate them within a long chronology. We nevertheless had to content ourselves primarily with foundations and vestigial paving, although in a few rare instances the elevation survived to a height of a few inches.

Above:
Foundation deposit found at the southwest corner of the Thutmose IV temple

Right:
Faience plaques from the foundation deposit, bearing the names of Thutmose III and Thutmose IV

Analysis and detailed diagramming of these remnants soon supplied basic documentation, making it possible to discern the series of walls and contemporaneous masonry. By assessing orientations and certain alignments, we managed to reconstitute one of the first edifices, a structure thirty-six meters long and over eleven meters wide. We therefore knew we were dealing with an Egyptian temple in Nubia that was remarkable in its layout and size. However, initially the possibilities for dating it were very limited, especially since certain architectural elements had to be dissociated from the main building being excavated. Pottery provided data confirming the date of one or several construction campaigns during the early Eighteenth Dynasty. However, examination of the southwest corner of the foundation ditch

The three-chambered sanctuary
and transversal corridor

of this structure revealed a major surprise: a few inscribed little plaques and beads of faience, along with models of pottery vessels, indicated that we had uncovered a foundation deposit of Thutmose IV.

The southern end of this temple was occupied by a three-chambered sanctuary, as were most religious buildings in Nubia, so the foundation deposit came from an outer corner of that sanctuary. When the enormous stone blocks of the wall were salvaged, the ditch into which these votive objects had been placed was partially disturbed. It was therefore important to dig out the southwest corner to confirm this initial chronological landmark, which in fact uncovered a second, intact, deposit below the base of the still-preserved foundation. This second deposit contained over fifty miniature pottery vessels and thirteen small faience plaques bearing the birth and throne names of Thutmose IV. Many beads were scattered in this very deep ditch. Three small faience plaques in the name of Thutmose III, found in the

first deposit, established a link with the earlier temple—Thutmose IV probably wanted to invoke the accomplishments of his grandfather.

The temple is entered from the paved path leading from the ceremonial palace (see diagram on page 48). The gateway, paved with enormous slabs of sandstone, boasted a stone-frame door that has now vanished. On either side, the clay soil bears marks of the first courses of a thin, long pylon, some twenty-five meters across and over three meters thick. The slow unearthing and drawing of each brick revealed that this pylon corresponded to the first level of paving, and that it was covered by other structures. Fragments of brickwork found at some depth make it possible to reconstitute the lateral walls of a quadrangular courtyard with longitudinal colonnades. Two column bases, the only ones to survive, have a diameter of forty centimeters and were therefore not suited to bear a roof of heavy slabs. The width of the central space in relation to the lateral bays also indicates that the longitudinal span was open to the sky. The two colonnades ended with the bases of two square pillars at the south end. In the middle was a paved surface five meters square. Just south were heavy foundations that certainly supported a door.

A very deep excavation in the middle is harder to interpret. The master builder called for ditches running over two meters deep, the lower part of which is filled with fine, sifted sand. Enormous blocks were placed on this bed. The surface of the blocks display engraved lines indicating the position of the next course. The plan that they suggest is irregular, and must reflect at least two different phases of construction. This plan was not conceived along a longitudinal axis and might suit the outline of the walls of four little side chambers. However, since these foundations obviously remain below the floor level of the building we might also interpret them as a system designed to support heavy architraves, the lower blocks serving as foundation piers. This second architectural option suggests that the area should be reconstituted as a hypostyle hall with a heavy roof that would have required such a foundation. From this hall we then move into a vestibule or court, wider than it is long, that leads into the sanctuary.

The tripartite sanctuary is preceded by a transversal corridor that provides access to each of the three chapels. All have the same dimensions, but it seems the two side chapels had not been paved. The central chapel, in contrast, had a floor of large blocks apparently designed to support the base of a probable naos. We were able to establish the partition walls, thanks to setting lines visible on the surface of the first course. While it is true that some of the blocks at the southwest corner are missing, the imprints of large stones indicate general alignments. An enclosing wall,

The often-restored sacred lake

renovated several times, has been located around the sanctuary and along the west wall of the temple—it would have isolated the building from all surrounding activities. Grains were transported into this sector and bread was prepared for offerings as indicated by the presence of numerous silos and secondary structures. To the east, we also noted the presence of layers of bread molds that had been discarded after use.

The temple built by Thutmose IV can be linked to the hydraulic installations to the north, where the ceremonial staircase had to be taken to reach the sacred lake or well near the western pier of the pylon. It is likely that direct access was arranged between the outer courtyard of the temple and the sacred lake, where water was sought after. Vestiges of an often-modified side-gate make it possible to reconstruct this route. Nearer the sanctuary, significantly thick walls replaced the structures used for private cults, probably in relation to the southern well. A room endowed

with a whitewashed floor occupied a rather large surface area, and apparently replaced an earlier arrangement. As for the southern well, it could certainly be reached by the underground passage that must still have been in use, although other prior installations were modified and razed. (It is worth noting that the eastern temple was also in use during this time.)

The side wall of the western temple, dated to the reign of Thutmose III, was contemporaneous with two transversal walls of mud brick, which turn to the east, where there runs a second side wall whose thickness should be revealed in future digs. Thutmose IV's rebuilt hypostyle hall and sanctuary were therefore set almost exactly in the middle of the mud-brick constructions of earlier kings. However, the transition to a building in which stone is more widely used obliged the architect to alter overall dimensions, by diminishing the width of the building and the thickness of walls. It is also likely that the first court and pylon underwent transfor-

Left:
Stela dedicated to Amun
Lord of Pnubs

Right:
Exterior view, temple
of Amada

Below:
Overall view of
the temple of Amun

mations, but the construction campaigns are hard to distinguish. Perhaps it was simply a question of making the existing court more monumental. It is the passage from this court and the potential hypostyle hall that might attest to two states of a northward extension.

Although none of the royal names found on the hundreds of limestone blocks and shards from this temple were sufficiently preserved to allow positive recognition of Thutmose IV rather than some other Thutmosid ruler, no traces of chiseling are detectable in the fragments of titularies

recovered. Deities identifiable by face or headdress represent one or several forms of falcon-headed Horus or tall-plumed Amun. The end of the god's name survives twice on the same block where it was carefully obliterated but can nevertheless still be clearly distinguished. This block, which was probably placed in line with the main sanctuary, provides proof, if needed, that the temple was dedicated to Amun. Many pieces of evidence of private worship of Amun were found in the hall located to the west of the temple. One of them, dating from the early Eighteenth

Dynasty, consists of a small stelae dedicated by an overseer of the stables of the Lord of the Two Lands to Amun-Re, Lord of P[n]ubs ('of the jujube tree').

The name of Thutmose IV has appeared fairly frequently in Nubia: on a stela and on seals of earthenware jars at Buhen, on a statuette at Gebel Barkal, and, in various places, on blocks reused in later temples or on bas-reliefs still in situ. The example of building B 600 at Gebel Barkal provides a significant general chronology, but the excavation carried out by George Reisner was not exhaustive. One can nevertheless see that the site was already occupied at the time of the Kerma civilizations, probably during the Classic Kerma Period considering the rectangular ditches of the two graves uncovered. A temple ten to fifteen meters long and roughly nine meters wide was erected in front of the rocky face of the sacred mount of Gebel Barkal, the foundation was likely constructed during the reign of Thutmose IV as suggested by a disturbed deposit located in the northeast corner of the main hall. In it are two small faience plaques inscribed with the king's name along with at least twelve miniature vessels very similar to those found in the Doukki Gel deposits.

The walls of Meroitic temple B 600 built on that spot include re-employed decorated stones among which Reisner not only recognized the characteristic use of gray sandstone but also identified the name of

Thutmose IV. Furthermore, analysis of the foundations showed that part of the masonry pre-dated the Meroitic Period. A nearby temple, B 700, was completely rebuilt during the reign of the early Napatan kings, but several older installations have been identified at the lower level. We feel it is particularly significant that the early Eighteenth Dynasty structures in this sector of Gebel Barkal are associated with the presence of a paved path identical to the one uncovered at Doukki Gel. The same type of paving and the construction of low walls abutting the flagstones have been observed; the segment of path studied does not, unfortunately, allow it to be linked to specific buildings.

Such comparisons begin to display some striking convergences of archaeological data. On the most sacred site in Nubia we find New Kingdom construction that seemed to mark a phase of development that had been preceded by other, earlier

foundations. Thutmose IV did not build on central locations, but rather in a sector threatened by falling rocks. He clearly wanted to get as close as possible to the cliff face and a venerated temple nearby, one probably erected by his forebear, Thutmose III, as attested by a stela.

More traces of major building work by Thutmose IV have also been found at the site of Tabo, some two hundred kilometers downstream from Gebel Barkal. Dozens of stones dating from the New Kingdom and decorated with wonderful bas-reliefs were retained in the walls of a temple built during the reign of a Twenty-fifth Dynasty ruler, Taharqa. These blocks, scattered throughout the lower courses of both pylons and in the walls of the hypostyle hall and sanctuary, had previously been used in temples whose location has not been pinpointed but which must have been in roughly the same location. A cartouche with the name of Thutmose IV was found,

and other reliefs are probably attributable to his reign.

In Lower Nubia, a temple at Amada still boasts splendid polychrome decoration in the classical Egyptian tradition. Its remarkable condition provides information on the archaeological evolution of a building erected under Thutmose III and his son Amenhotep II, ultimately completed in the third year of this latter king's reign, as mentioned on a stela in the temple. Additions by Thutmose IV must correspond to two campaigns of renovation of the courtyard, rapidly transformed into a hypostyle hall. A set of twelve pillars was thus added in front of a portico present from the start. The two rows of outer pillars were re-carved in order to insert the lateral panels connecting them. These pillars naturally evoke the colonnade of the festival court that Thutmose IV erected in front of the fourth pylon at Karnak. Also worth mentioning are the many fragments of pillars

recovered at Doukki Gel, including one very fine example depicting the face of Horus on two contiguous sides.

As we can see, the temple of Amun Lord of Pnubs is a major Nubian monument. It fits into a well-attested chronology that begins with work carried out on a significant scale under Thutmose III and Amenhotep II, followed in turn by Thutmose IV who respected his predecessors' decisions even as he revised the overall archaeological scheme. It is worth stressing that the plan he elaborated already appeared highly classical, and it would be largely imitated during the remainder of the New Kingdom. Also worth noting is the unusual breadth of the pylon, whose piers extend far beyond the lateral walls, giving it unusual proportions. This design perhaps represented a mud-brick adaptation of a model generally witnessed in structures of stone. Even though pylons progressively became a regular feature of most temples, the final form of the pylon had not yet been established.

Stone pendant, proof of a private cult practiced to the west of the temple

Akhenaten at Pnubs

Excavation of the eastern temple of Doukki Gel brought to light the remains of stone paving that had been disturbed by the ditches dug by *sebbakhin*. This paving was contemporaneous with a Napatan religious building and had been laid in the halls that preceded the sanctuary. This discovery acquired additional interest when we noticed well-preserved details of iconography and inscriptions on the stones. Furthermore, these stones were so uniform that we immediately identified them as *talatat*, the term used by residents of the village of Karnak to describe blocks of sandstone cut into fifty-two by twenty-seven by twenty-two centimeter pieces. Stones of this size could be carried by a single man, which thereby sped up construction. Traces of plaster indicated that irregularities in the stone, hewed fairly quickly in the quarry, were remedied with thick joins and fillings. It therefore seemed certain that a temple to Aten had been built here during the reign of Akhenaten. However, no traces of that edifice could be discerned on the spot.

One year later, an extension of the dig zone revealed that a second temple occupied the area that ran westward to the precinct wall, and that the *talatat* were incorporated into its foundations. The

Talatat stones used for the floor of the eastern temple

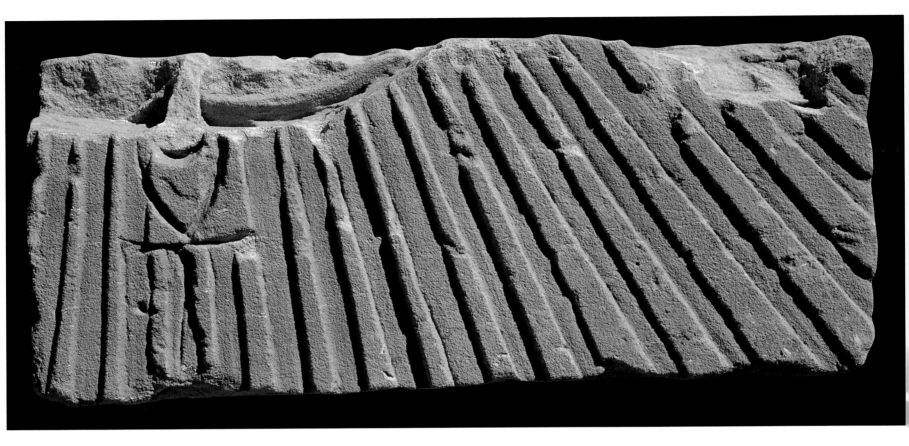

Top:
Aten's disk and solar rays

Above:
The names of Aten in two
cartouches

discovery of the foundation deposit of Thutmose IV provided proof that the same temple predated the transfer of the Egyptian capital to al-Amarna. The accession of the king known as Amenhotep IV occurred at Thebes; five years into his seventeen-year reign he began calling himself Akhenaten and moved to his new capital with his queen, Nefertiti. This move reflected profound changes, for it was also decreed that the Egyptian pantheon would be replaced by a single god, Aten. The architectural programs undertaken at Thebes and then at al-Amarna reflected the unprecedented activity that occurred during that period. The religious revolution triggered by the king was accompanied by the birth of a startling school of art, whose quality has often been stressed. Depictions of the king and queen beneath the rays of the sun terminating in a hand holding the *ankh,* or symbol of life, imposed an ideal image that nevertheless embodied a realism directly related to the reforms that stemmed from the monarch's ideology.

This extraordinary period required Egyptian architects to implement new techniques to replace all houses of worship

of Amun by grand sanctuaries dedicated to the one god, Aten. We have little information on the state of temples abandoned or transformed, because these activities primarily involved new establishments, as mentioned on the thousands of *talatat* later reused in subsequent buildings. At least eight temples have been identified at Thebes, and their dimensions appear to have been considerable. The same is true at al-Amarna, where the largely excavated foundations reveal the vast plan of Akhenaten's incomparable city. The fact that we found traces of a temple so removed from that capital, all the way into Upper Nubia,

was exceptional in itself, but being able to study the reconstruction of Thutmose IV's temple at Doukki Gel in order to adapt it to the worship of Aten represented a truly unique opportunity. We therefore sought to uncover all clues relating to the Amarna Period, while simultaneously studying the way in which the building campaign might have been conducted.

Overall observations showed that the previous temple had been completely razed. A few elements of the foundations were nevertheless retained over the entire construction zone. In the sanctuary, for instance, a single course had been pre-

served, and on its surface was the plaster that cemented the *talatat*. On some of the large blocks laid by Thutmose IV there arose stonework done entirely with *talatat*. Cross-section digs into demolition strata confirmed that the stone blocks comprising the walls of Thutmose's temple were cut down into small fragments and shards; many of those fragments still bore traces of inscriptions or carved and painted decoration. It has been demonstrated that part of this work was done in order to cut the temple blocks into *talatat* for reuse, yet we also have proof that the bases of supports were broken up with no identifiable goal of

The reuse of earlier stones
for the temple of Aten

pavement with stones, worn and reused, that were not as homogeneous as those used in the earlier paving.

The mud-brick pylon was razed down to the second course, and the new Amarnian construction altered the appearance of the entrance entirely. An impressive new gate was erected, each of its quadrangular piers measuring seven by eight meters. The doorway, approximately 2.75 meters wide, was defined by two rows of *talatat* that lined the mud-brick piers. The totally modified dimensions of the pylon lent the gate a similarity to ones seen in Amarnian depictions. It is interesting to note the added thickness of the pylon—both in front and behind the older gate—probably designed to achieve greater height, which better suited its slightly sloping walls (see diagram on page 57).

The first courtyard, located just behind this pylon-like structure, must have had two lateral colonnades at that time. One of these columns' bases has been found in situ, with remnants of plaster used to set the first drum; it measures 1.20 meters in diameter, which shows just how strong the columns must have been. At roughly one meter in diameter, they could be expected to support a roof made of slabs of stone. The surface of the ground was probably strengthened by *talatat* that have now somewhat disintegrated. Foundations of mud brick and fragmented sandstone at the location of the columns have made it possible to reconstitute the northern end, but the southernmost support structures are missing. Also in this area, a transversal passage was created with doors that cut through each of the side walls of mud brick. The east door, with a stone architrave, led to a colonnaded courtyard and the neighboring temple. The doorway to the west, which has retained its infrastructure of sandstone blocks, led into a very long chapel. The contemporaneous layers of this chapel have not yet been excavated, but

potential reuse. Exploitation of the masonry of Thutmose IV's temple left countless heaps of rubble, so it was upon a layer of fragments of gray sandstone some forty to fifty centimeters thick that Akhenaten's construction work began.

The subsequent course of construction becomes harder to understand once we note that a series of substantial posts apparently copy the former plan along several lines. Thus after leveling the existing temple entirely, the master builder seems to have sought to preserve some of the main axes and the positions of certain walls, quickly rebuilt from *talatat*. The vestiges of an oven set into the first courtyard relate to this stage of renovation, as does a votive deposit under one of the uprights of a side door to the east of the court. The deposit contained a bird-shaped alabaster dish that was placed alongside two large earthenware jars and a seal; additional pottery vessels were placed around this group. The path leading to the entrance gate of the temple was also partly copied, but raising the ground level required laying new

Two jars from the foundation deposit

The Amarnian foundation deposit placed beneath a doorpost

a great number of fragmentary statues from various periods have been recovered from the Meroitic levels.

In the middle of the temple we once again come across the excavation that we linked to the foundations of a hypostyle hall. Strangely, a deeply buried wall incorporates older side structures. Farther south, other elevated sections of *talatat* show that the earlier foundations helped to support new constructions. Prior foundations had to bear elements of the intermediate gate between the court and the central section of the temple. Farther along, a second court might have been occupied by some of the increasingly numerous altars in Amarnian temples—at least two distinct masonry structures rise above the floor level of the *talatat*. The sanctuary, meanwhile, must have been completely rebuilt, and the paving of the main chapel was covered; in the access corridor and the chambers themselves it can be seen how the rows of *talatat* were employed, sometimes extending beyond the edges of the earlier foundations. So despite a thorough construction campaign that modified the overall building, the initial architectural structure was partly respected in a clear desire to ensure certain continuity.

Amenhotep III's grandiose architectural projects at Soleb and Sedeinga signify the pharaoh's interest in Nubia. Knowing the close relationship between the king and his son, Amenhotep IV (Akhenaten), it is not surprising that this policy continued into the next reign. However, it should be remembered that the temple at Soleb was modified during the Amarna Period. In the outer hall and around the gate of the large pylon, Akhenaten had his two cartouches carved on top of those of Amenhotep III. The transformation of the temple entrance—and probably also the similarly aligned gateway between the first and second courts—provides evidence of

The central section of the temple
of Aten

Right: The main temple at Sesebi,
built under Amenhotep IV and
renovated by Sety I

Vestiges of the sanctuary rebuilt during
the reign of Akhenaten

an operation identical to the one carried out at Doukki Gel, most likely to create monumental open-topped gates.

Tangible proof of continuity between the reigns of Amenhotep III and Amenhotep IV (Akhenaten) can be seen in the founding of the town of Sesebi. Located fifty kilometers south of Soleb and forty kilometers north of Kerma, this settlement covered an area of 270 by 200 meters ringed by a fortified wall defended by rectangular bastions. The town was later extended in the direction of the Nile. A terrace in the north sector of town was designed to take a triple temple; foundation deposits in the name of Amenhotep IV have been linked to it. The base supporting the religious complex was composed of rough-hewn building stones that might have been prepared for another, prior project that was never completed. A smaller solar temple was built some distance away, in the same precinct. Extensions made to the main complex with *talatat* point to later work carried out under Akhenaten.

The town of Kawa, located fifty kilometers upstream of Kerma, bore the ancient name of Gem-Aten ('he who finds the disk'), which implies the existence of an Amarnian establishment, now echoed only by the presence of a temple of Tutankhamun. The same uncertainty recurs at Gebel Barkal, where *talatat* have been found but whose provenance has yet to be established. The discovery of a temple to Aten at Doukki Gel lends greater scope to the spread of the worship of a single god glorified by the solar disk. Amenhotep IV was already pursuing his father's ambitious architectural policies in the early part of his reign, as illustrated by the fortified town of Sesebi. The systematic demolition of the temple of Amun of Pnubs came at a later stage, once the Aten schism had occurred. And it might be imagined that such operations continued southward, for navigation

on the Nile—once the third cataract had been passed—made movement much easier. Gebel Barkal's reputation as a center of the Amun cult must also have spurred Akhenaten to transform this holy site to the worship of Aten.

The role of Akhenaten's emissaries to Kerma must have fulfilled two imperatives. On the one hand, they embodied a policy of occupying lands where disturbances were always possible, and on the other hand they had to promote the spread of a highly original, exclusive religion that would not necessarily be accepted unhesitatingly by people who had long been worshiping Amun. At both Sesebi and Doukki Gel there were clearly efforts to fortify the town. On the latter site, the alterations to the temple do not suggest a complete abandonment of the roof covering the central section and sanctuary. We are therefore faced with a building that differed from the architectural reconstructions at al-Amarna and Thebes, where the temples were left open to the sky and were entirely devoted to the solar cult, which basically performed services in the open air. At Sesebi both of these tendencies can be detected, with a solar platform and a triple building composed of several roofed rooms. The decoration of the temple at Doukki Gel, meanwhile, was quite similar to those found on some of the temples in Karnak. It included large scenes of offerings beneath the omnipresent solar disk, and outlines of figures wrapped in flowing garments of transparent linen, so typical of Amarna art. As with earlier temples, this decoration was executed by teams who traveled down from Egypt.

Once the Amarna Period had come to an end, the royal faces and names on the temple's bas-reliefs were chiseled out, which indicates that the building remained standing for some time. Various clues suggest that the reliefs were later covered with plaster and at least partly re-carved. That work was

probably undertaken by King Sety I, whose name is mentioned on a building stone. Sesebi also displays evidence of work by Sety I, who was possibly trying to re-establish orthodoxy throughout the region. The first court of the temple at Doukki Gel, meanwhile, received pillars set on a foundation of *talatat* that evoke these changes. Although it is in the sanctuary zone that Sety's campaign is most clear: extreme pillaging and salvaging of stone heavily affected this sanctuary, which hardly facilitates an exact analysis of successive modifications. One old *talatat* found in this sector was plastered and re-carved with the depiction of a king accompanied by the commander of the Kush regiment, Bakensetekh, probably contemporaneous with the reign of Ramesses III. This discovery tends to prove that the building was still in use toward the end of the New Kingdom.

Top:
Obliterated profile of Queen Nefertiti

Above:
Talatat reused during the Ramesside Period

The Kushite Temples of Pnubs

We have already mentioned the extent to which the Twenty-fifth Dynasty represented a period of renewal in Nubia. Everywhere, large buildings were erected and the monarchs enjoyed unrivaled power. However, apart from a few stones with fine decoration and an attestation that King Shabaqo was the builder, excavations at Doukki Gel have not turned up many well-dated vestiges still in their original locations. The majority of sculpted stones from that period was found in layers of Meroitic demolition rubble or in a bench placed in front the Napatan pylon at the eastern temple. And we also noticed that the transversal chapel of the eastern temple contains foundation stones hewn in a way identical to those used in the main building at Tabo erected by Taharqa. It was Taharqa, and one of his predecessors, Piankhy, who set up the two granite blocks in the sanctuary of temple B 500 at Gebel Barkal. These monumental bases are similar to the ones found in the eastern temple at Doukki Gel.

This temple was probably rebuilt during the Napatan Period, replacing a Twenty-fifth Dynasty edifice whose stone walls were completely reused. The later Napatan plan comprised a pylon that was not very thick and a very large gate opening onto a hall with four columns partly salvaged from a New Kingdom building. The walls were raised in mud brick, although all the door jambs are in sandstone. That was also the case for the west door to the next room, which led toward the temple of Amun. A third room occupied the entire width of the temple, but was not very long. The sanctuary can only be reconstituted by reference to the two granite bases. A series of roofed rooms with aligned passages leading to a

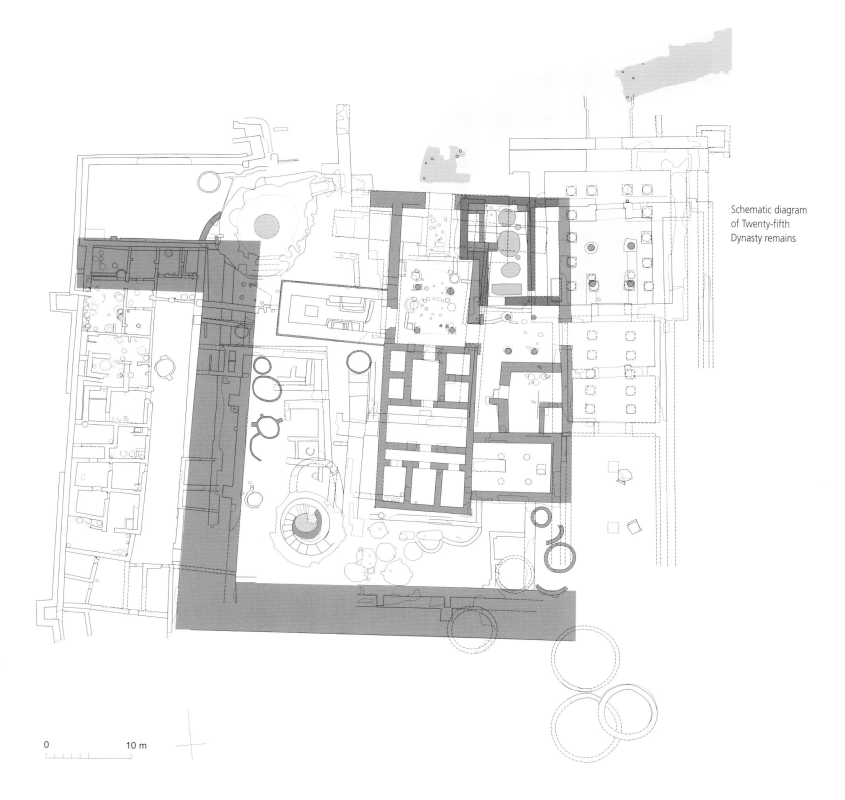

Schematic diagram
of Twenty-fifth
Dynasty remains

0   10 m

Excavation of part of
the L-shaped room

Left:
Aerial view of the Napato-
Meroitic temple at Doukki
Gel in the early stages of
excavation

The three circular pits in the L-shaped room

Fragment of a Ramesses II stela

space where the first base was located, followed by a three-chambered sanctuary, was common in Nubian regions. It can be seen as a local adaptation of Egyptian architecture, clearly articulated at Gebel Barkal during that period.

In the next-door temple, dedicated to Amun Lord of Pnubs, an unusual feature must certainly be dated, through relative chronology, to the Twenty-fifth Dynasty and the Napatan Period. This feature included an L-shaped room that occupied the site of the eastern pier of the pylon and extended toward the south, plus a very long and narrow adjoining room that abutted the lateral wall of the eastern temple (see diagram on page 65). The mud-brick construction was very meticulous. The L-shaped room had a large door at south end, while a secondary door led into the adjoining room. The outer wall, which doubled as the façade of the temple, turned back along the entrance passage and then ran around the colonnaded court. The master builder thereby expressed a determination to incorporate this new suite into the two temples. This was further reinforced by the creation of a passageway between the two temples, in front of the entrance to the L-shaped room, via a court also flanked by two colonnades.

The L-shaped room was furnished with benches or bases of mud brick. At the foot of the L, next to the temple gate, there was a kind of solid coffer on which ritual implements could be stored. Three roundish pits and one rectangular pit were dug into the compact clay ground. While the central pit, three meters in diameter, contained the primary cache, the others were filled differently. The oval pit to the south yielded limited material in soil that was not very compact, though a fragment of a fine stela of Ramesses II was found in it, along with other, undecorated stones. In front of the door, a sort of test pit was also filled with loose earth and several pieces of a large sandstone offering

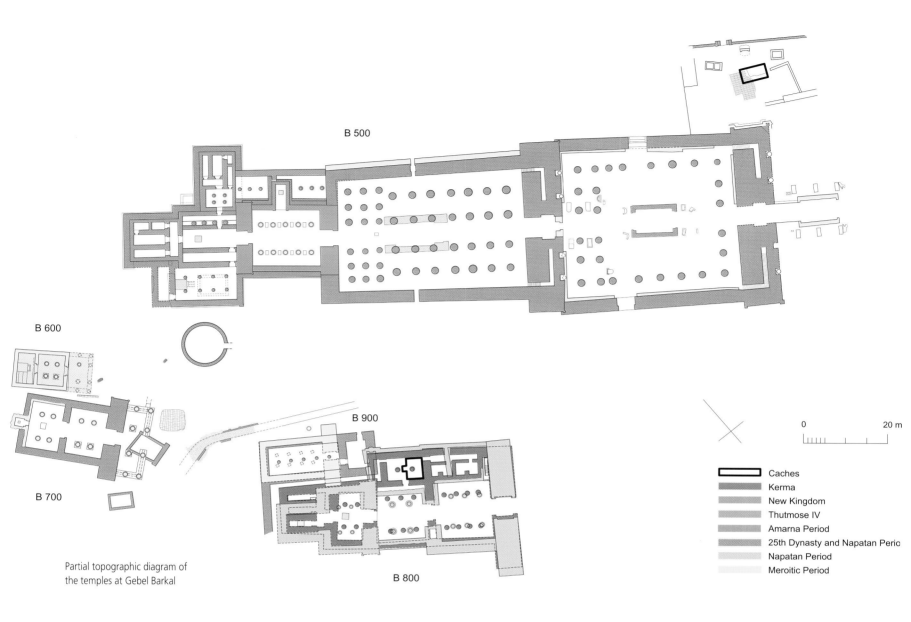

B 500

B 600

B 700

B 900

B 800

Partial topographic diagram of
the temples at Gebel Barkal

0   20 m

▭ Caches
▓ Kerma
▓ New Kingdom
▓ Thutmose IV
▓ Amarna Period
▓ 25th Dynasty and Napatan Perio
▓ Napatan Period
▓ Meroitic Period

table. The round pit to the north, which seems to have been sealed with a cover of hardened clay, was difficult to excavate, and the result of our efforts turned out to be disappointing: extremely hard layers yielded only a few potshards, mainly from the Classic Kerma Period but also from the Middle Kerma era.

As just described, it was mainly in the longer part of the L that we discovered traces of use; the foot of the L, to the west, was probably assigned another role. At the south end the ground had often been dug up, and analysis of alterations to the entrance door suggests that the L-shaped room was predated by a smaller room from New Kingdom days. The function of this smaller room, which assumed sufficient importance during the Napatan Period to be used for a sacred deposit, can perhaps be

understood in light of similar caches uncovered by George Reisner at Gebel Barkal. Comparison reveals several points of similarity, especially since the deposits of broken statues include the same kings found at Doukki Gel. The two Gebel Barkal deposits were contemporaneous, and fragments of the statues were divided between the caches. The caches were thus prepared at the same moment, and the fragments of statues were distributed in these two known points with no concern for reassembly of their constituent elements. Reisner proposed a single original location for the statues, namely one of the courts of Gebel Barkal's main temple, B 500, which was flanked by the two caches, thereby facilitating the disposal operation.

The many Twenty-fifth Dynasty buildings at Gebel Barkal studied by the early

American excavators constitute a major source of information. Yet despite very careful digging, it is extremely difficult to follow the transformations of the edifices and to assign them precise dates; the temples known as B 800 and B 900 offer good examples. The former originally featured a tripartite sanctuary and a hall with four columns. Alongside it was another hall with a single row of columns, preceded by a vestibule, which was transformed into a temple (B 900) during a later phase (see diagram on page 67). B 800 was enlarged with a pylon and two courts with lateral colonnades. The second court met a hall with two columns, accompanied by several small rooms that lined the outer walls of the courts. It was in this hall, situated between the second court of B 800 and the approach to the entrance of B 900, that one of the caches of statues was deposited right on the paving and then covered with a fairly homogeneous fill. Access to this cache was therefore through the court of B 800, and not from the outside, directly from main temple B 500.

This latter temple, B 500, can be linked to the second cache. Outside and slightly beyond the first pylon, built during Piankhy's reign, the vestiges of a Twenty-fifth Dynasty building were found—probably one connected to the temple. The building was demolished, but its floor, composed of large slabs of whitish sandstone, has partly survived. The work of preparing a pit underneath this paving was carried out in order to house fragments of statues, which were placed in the hole on top of the remains of the paving stones. On this spot, then, there was an edifice of a certain size that could be accessed from the courtyard

of temple B 500. This building must have existed prior to the burial of the statues and has been chosen as the removal point for broken colossi that were cluttering the space(s) where they formerly stood. Both of these spots represent examples, as does the L-shaped room in Doukki Gel, of premises accessible from—yet independent of—colonnaded courts.

Once the dating of the L-shaped room was established, an exploratory dig was conducted in the western coffer where the construction protruded. The upper layers yielded a certain quantity of gold leaf still stuck to plaster. It was apparent that the preparatory plaster had been applied to fabric, for the regular weave left an imprint. We assumed that we had come across a gold store or collection of precious objects. A bronze statue of a Meroitic king, uncovered in the court of the temple at

Tabo, displayed the same handling of the surface, if at a much later date. In order to avoid dangerous haste and to prepare the next stage of operations, work was halted in this zone. It only began again two years later, once we were in possession of additional chronological data.

The excavation of the L-shaped room then became a high priority, because we sensed that these pieces of gold leaf, deliberately left there, must belong to a most unusual deposit. It was necessary to cut stratigraphic sections in the ground in order to fully perceive the layers of infill. This zone had been damaged in antiquity, since the holes were clearly detectible on the surface. Around the door, however, there remained some paving stones, and we realized that this paving had been removed during construction work in the room, and that most of the slabs had never

Aerial view of
the temple at Tabo

Statue of a Meroitic king during restoration of the layer of plaster and gold leaf that covered it

been replaced. Since the location of the round pits had been obvious from an early date, we decided to excavate only one half of each hole, in order to study the cross-sections by leaving one of the sides intact. Although the archaeological yield on the surface was relatively insignificant, the central pit quickly began producing a large quantity of gold leaf and an accumulation of fragments of plaster. The cross-section made it possible to follow the inclined strata, revealing how the infill had been placed in a series of successive deposits. It became apparent that the gilded objects had originally been installed in the western part of the L-shaped room, and then carried to the central pit, along with the resulting debris of such an operation.

A Virgin Cache

On January 11, 2003, a finely polished fragment of granite emerged in the northern half of the central pit. Slightly inclined, its long surface had been carefully engraved—we were soon able to read two cartouches bearing the name of King Taharqa. At first sight, the granite pillar seemed to be a monumental doorpost, but steady excavation revealed the pleats of a pharaoh's kilt. We then realized we were in the presence of the rear pillar of a statue, this 1.5 meter section representing just the main trunk. The perfect proportions of the piece underscored the importance of the find, especially since the remarkably preserved carving indicated the skill of the workshop that had produced it. We were immediately struck by the polish on this hard stone, which usually degrades quickly during extended transportation or constant moves. The digging continued slowly downward, steadily uncovering the monarch's strong arm and wrist, which—even though the statue had been broken at the level of the head and the knees—still conveyed all his might.

Excavation was slowed by a profusion of gold leaf and plaster that had clearly been part of a decorative feature applied to the statue. In certain cases, we had the impression that some of the pieces were still stuck to the stone, yet we were unable to provide absolute proof of it. Soon the presence of two other statues, lying directly to the south of the first, impressed upon us the import of the contents of the pit: it was a deposit of several royal statues, a practice that had been attested elsewhere. We immediately realized that this cache represented a significant moment in the history of the site of Doukki Gel, and that it was crucial that

Back pillar of the statue of Taharqa during excavation

Head of one of the statues of King
Tanutamun in situ

we do our utmost to preserve all data relating to the archaeological context of the discovery. Thus every fragment was left in its original position, awaiting the complete excavation of the pit and a detailed recording of it, in order to transmit a faithful image of this virgin cache to both specialists and general public alike. Furthermore, in order to protect the polished surfaces and the broken fragments, which were highly fragile, excavators were instructed not to lean on the pieces of carved stone that took up nearly all the available space. Digging thus became an acrobatic feat.

The bodies of two other statues, partially embedded into the stratigraphic section, were of equally great interest. One was the bust of a king dressed in a panther skin, the other was a large piece of the back pillar of a statue immediately identifiable, thanks to three of his names, as the last king of the Twenty-fifth Dynasty: Tanutamun. By digging behind the chest of the other king and using a piece of mirror, we were able to glimpse the Horus name used by King Senkamanisken. Thus we began to anticipate—and to hope for—a direct analogy with the caches found by Reisner at Gebel Barkal, which also contained broken statues of these same three kings. The potential repetition of an identical find at Kerma, located at the other end of the Kushite kingdom, lent the phenomenon new historical scope. Taking these initial results into account, daily work proceeded very slowly on the first half of the pit. Many fragments that lay completely on the bottom, at the natural ground level some two meters down, steadily came to light.

Although several smaller, irregular fragments occupied much of the space, we were fascinated above all by a splendid head that was resting near the body of Tanutamun. The soft light of early after-

noon revealed features of startling, almost oriental, purity. Two other heads, nestled beneath the arm of King Taharqa, were also of great quality. One of the headdresses still bore a tiny piece of plaster and gold-leaf. Other fragments, representing more or less whole legs and arms, were arrayed at the bottom of the cache. A small sculpture carved in gray sandstone stood out from the fragments of harder stone, which were dark gray or black. Whereas the first phase of digging had turned up relatively large components, the lower part of the pit contained smaller fragments scattered among the larger ones. One false move might destroy them forever, especially since the violent blows that shattered the statues had already weakened these fragments most.

After this first stage of excavation, it was necessary to draw and photograph the overall state of things, after a lengthy cleaning process. These visual documents would allow us to consider the situation carefully before excavating any further. We also wanted to inform the authorities and local residents. Indeed, for many years we have been making regular presentations of our discoveries in response to the interest displayed by people. But the management of hundreds of visitors who began arriving after a broadcast on Sudanese television, which had to be coordinated with protection of the site, and in which the police and army quickly became involved, inevitably complicated our work. Examination of the statues also indicated that some of the fragments were of considerable weight—from one to two tons—which would require special techniques for lifting and transporting them. In a region where mechanical equipment is not readily available, we had to devise a system that would be simple. It was essential that our design help us to prevent further damage to the stones and avoid any accident during the operations.

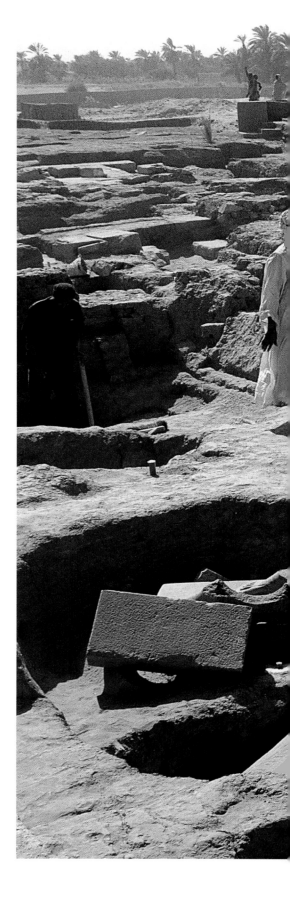

Shortly after the discovery,
visitors showed great interest

The head of Taharqa in situ

Right:
The bases of the statues were grouped together at the top of one side of the pit

After a visit by several ministers and officials from Sudan's Department of Antiquities, the next stage of excavation could begin on the second half of the pit. Sculpted stone appeared almost immediately below the surface—it turned out to be two bases for the statues of Taharqa and Tanutamun. The base for Taharqa's statue was large and carved with great care. The craftsmanship revealed the elegance of the feet and the details on the sandals, leather straps decorated with a winged scarab. The king's feet were trampling the Nine Bows, representing the countries subject to his authority. The other base was upside-down, but the inscription engraved on top could just be glimpsed: it named Tanutamun. A third

base, leaning against the south wall of the pit, also bore Tanutamun's names, it was becoming clear that some kings were represented twice. On the east side of the pit we could see a fourth base, and we suspected a fifth one was laying beneath Taharqa's base. Two other plinths were deposited in the north half, which meant that the cache contained at least seven statues. The bases were primarily found in the upper layer, so they must have been deposited during the last phase of the procedure.

This general arrangement, with the bodies of the various statues lying in the intermediate strata, was fairly typical. To prevent the heavy bases on top from tumbling, only the lateral parts were scraped

away. A test dig to the east, along the median section, brought to light the upper part of a head that was larger than the two heads already discovered. On carefully cleaning the face of this admirable sculpture, which was resting on the bottom of the pit, we began to recognize Taharqa's distinctive facial features. Furthermore, the dimensions of the head corresponded to the larger of the bodies already uncovered. Taking a few measurements on the spot, we were able to assign an approximate height of 2.7 meters to this statue. Here again, at certain times of the day the raking sunlight brought out the outstanding quality of the king's face, which had been particularly well preserved. On the other side of the pit, at almost the same time, we

uncovered a back pillar of the Nubian king Anlamani, which led us to believe that the pit still held major surprises.

Immediately next to the body of Anlamani, lying on its side, we soon came across the body of his successor, Aspelta, lying face up. Finding Aspelta convinced us that the Doukki Gel cache was almost exactly the same as the deposits found at Gebel Barkal. Further excavation in between the various fragments also brought to light four older sculptures, including a fine royal head and the lower part of a seated figure, both dating from the New Kingdom. A falcon head in sandstone and a fragment of a statuette of a woman holding a flower were some of the other sundry objects deposited with the royal statues.

Once the entire cache had been freed of loose infill, it became risky to dig any further, lest one of the big blocks should tumble. Furthermore, the perspective afforded by this view of the pit made it possible to analyze the interrelationships of the fragments and to grasp the relative order in which the pieces were deposited into the cache—the heads, for instance, were buried deeply, probably to protect them. More than at any other stage of the excavation, we realized how privileged we were to be studying this deposit intact, undisturbed since the sixth century BCE.

It was important to conserve this kind of ideal image not only through a photographic record as complete as possible but also through a large-scale drawing of each accessible piece. By using accurate reference points, a drawing made it possible to pinpoint their planar position with precision. Such work would continue throughout the disassembly of the cache, at different levels, in order to locate all the fragments according to the same reference points. This was naturally a slow process, but indispensable to a visual record of the entire cache. The experience of the members of the team

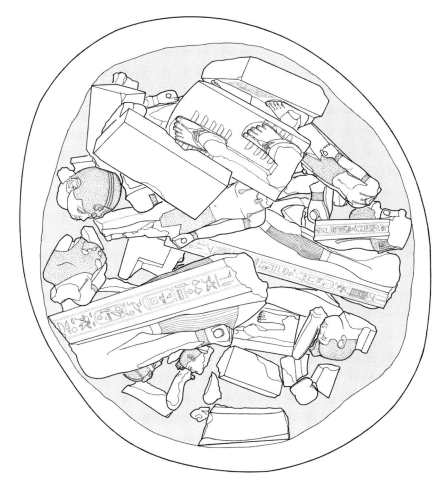

Detailed drawing of the cache
(upper level)

played a significant role in coordinating the successive operations. The work of the artists was constantly interrupted by the photographing of details as a function of changes in light throughout the day, which also meant getting the grid strings and work bench out of the way. The operation was made even more complicated by the anticipated and ultimately actual arrival of a large helicopter with a French television crew headed by Nicolas Hulot, who was preparing a broadcast on Sudan. The filming, in fact, turned out to be a useful addition to more traditional methods of recording the data, and the aerial photos taken from the helicopter contributed to a more thorough documentation of the site of Doukki Gel.

Emptying the cache of its contents required the installation of a hoist. Once fragments were hoisted out, a temporary

Far left:
The cache after excavation

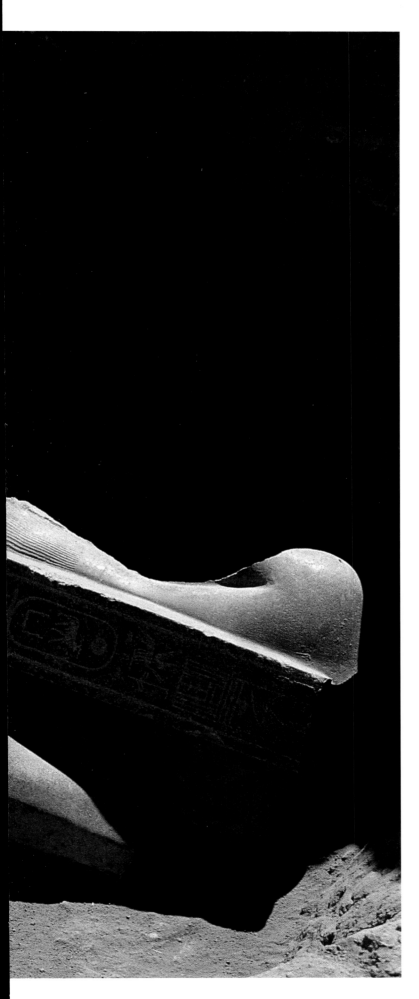

The cache after initial removal
of fragments

Detailed drawing of the cache
(lower level)

arrangement was devised to move them to a zone where the re-composition of the statues was also being organized—a system of wood boards on rollers, dragged over a long distance, took us back to operations of a bygone era. The most difficult thing, however, remained maneuvers within the pit, where fragments could not be allowed to come into unprotected contact with one another. This made us realize the care with which these fragments of statues had been moved in ancient times, when they were placed in the pit, because they bore almost no marks of damage when one piece was laid upon another—earth had been spread around to prevent the pieces from knocking each other and to facilitate putting them down. It was this earth-fill that contained the greatest amount of plaster and gold leaf. The plaster almost always had a smooth surface and had been applied to fabric, whose negative imprint had sometimes survived. Several small plaques of yellow glass, three centimeters square, and two small plaques of finely polished lapis lazuli must also have been part of the original decoration of these statues.

Once the four bases on top had been removed, renewed digging presented us with an improved view of the cache. Several body sections, partly hidden till then, became completely visible. A second statue of Senkamanisken was resting against the one of Anlamani, while fragments of the body of the second statue of Tanutamun were placed directly below them. As still-buried fragments came to light, one of the most moving moments was once again associated with a magnificent head, that of Anlamani. He was wearing the double crown of Egypt, which still retained a few traces of original color, and yet the most striking thing were the ram's horns that curled down either side of a face of almost unreal beauty. At the bot-

tom of the pit, once most of the fragments had been removed, we found the head of Senkamanisken, also wearing the double crown, covered in a coating of watery clay. These traces of liquid do not seem to have affected the entire pit and must have been caused when the hole was almost empty. Senkamanisken's head was the only one that turned out to be incomplete.

The bodies of Taharqa and Tanutamun, which were the heaviest pieces, were moved toward the end of the operation in order to benefit from our accumulating experience. All the tasks of lifting, moving, and adjusting the fragments were confided to a member of the team whose profession of sculptor gave him skills, acquired at Carrara, that were of particular value. While emptying the cache we had attempted to ascertain, despite the mutilations, whether many fragments were missing, but reassembly of the fifty-two pieces called for a fuller examination with the help of an accurate inventory of the fragments belonging to each of the henceforth identified statues. This was yet another delicate operation if we hoped to avoid damaging the thin edges of stone during handling. Furthermore, simply turning these heavy pieces in the sand might damage the quality of the high polish, which would lose its luster. The two heaviest statues were thus immediately placed in a warehouse built to that effect, while the five other royal statues were first studied in the open air. Reassembly soon showed that despite systematic breakage of heads, legs, and arms, very few fragments were actually missing.

Initial observations and analyses were thus greatly facilitated. Facsimiles of the inscription, begun in the pit itself for the heaviest pieces, were taken under better conditions on the reconstituted statues. The wealth of writing called for an extremely detailed transcription of the hieroglyphic signs, which in general were

The head of King Anlamani at the bottom of the pit

Raising the torso of the statue
of Taharqa

quite distinctly carved, except on the back pillar of Anlamani, where they were inscribed very superficially. When handling and assembling these fragments, the existence of very different stylistic influences became readily apparent. The influence of traditional Egyptian statuary was of course obvious, but several other artistic trends seem to have arisen during this period of upheaval along the Nile Valley. It is worth noting that when describing the black and gray stone of the statues we used the terms granite and gabbro, yet we remain ignorant for the moment of the provenance and morphological diversity of this rock. Some of the stones look as though they might have come from the third cataract, where there were quarries at Tumbus, some twenty kilometers away. Finally, we also noted the existence of a painted surface on several of the statues particularly that of Anlamani, entirely covered in a black wash.

It was crucial to prepare for subsequent operations on the site. We thought it reasonable to avoid lengthy transportation of the statues, during which the high polish, so well preserved up till then, might be scratched, or some of the fragile zones of fracture might be damaged. We therefore opted to reconstruct them at Kerma itself. Since a decision to found a museum on the site had already been the object of an official ceremony in the presence of members of the government, it was decided that the cache would remain at Kerma and be displayed there. The erection of the temporary warehouse, begun right from day one of the discovery, gave us sufficient time to accomplish our study of the statues and to devise a reassembly of the fragments with appropriate cement. The specialist we consulted demonstrated the complexity of an operation that included, for example, the cleaning of fractured rock that had acquired calcareous and saline deposits over the pre-

Reassembling one of the statues
of Tanutamun

ceding 2,500 years. Analysis of the surfaces was also crucial for recognizing the various substances applied to the rock.

The interest sparked by the discovery of this cache, both within Sudan and in the international press, spurred us to present the results of our work at Doukki Gel without further ado. The report was nevertheless designed above all to illustrate the stages in the discovery and opening of the cache. Photographs of the restored statues would not be available for several years. We therefore had to come up with an intermediate plan that would include photos giving a good idea of the high quality of these artworks. Despite a certain num-

ber of constraints, a photographic record was begun the following year, during a new phase of work, notwithstanding the difficulties of shifting the fragments in and out of the warehouse (with a ceiling somewhat low for the largest statues), and the problem of photographic lighting in natural light. During these operations an initial in-depth study could be carried out, contributing further observations to the preliminary study. Each working session that afforded us the opportunity to contemplate these statues revealed new, original features of the works and underscored their contribution to our knowledge of Kushite statuary.

THE ROYAL STATUES

The Statues of Taharqa and Tanutamun

Of the seven monumental standing statues of kings found in the cache at Doukki Gel, three belonged to the late Twenty-fifth Dynasty. Already profoundly influenced by their country's long incorporation and cultural assimilation into the Egyptian empire during the latter half of the second millennium BCE, the Kushite kings adopted the artistic criteria of the land they conquered in the eighth century BCE. In Egypt, the main canons of royal statuary had been laid down during the Fourth Dynasty, and they would remain almost unchanged up the Roman era, even if sculptors managed to display great inventiveness throughout the country's long history. The most ancient monumental in-the-round portraits of an Egyptian monarch are those showing Menkaure (Mycerinus), notably as part of a sculpted group. In the pair he forms with his queen (Museum of Fine Arts, Boston) and in the state triads where he is associated with the goddess Hathor and a personification of a province (Egyptian Museum, Cairo), we can already see the artistic criteria that would be reproduced, almost unchanging, for several thousand years: a frontal pose, broad shoulders, arms held tight against the sides, hands holding the *mekes* container (enclosing the papyrus roll on which is inscribed the property of Egypt); feet are set flat on the base with the left foot always placed forward, in a striding pose; the king's back often abuts a vertical support—slab, pillar or obelisk—which reinforces the physical solidity of the piece (for the same reasons, the left leg is incorporated into this support); the king always wears the pleated kilt that Egyptians called the *shendjyt*. Headdress and adornment might vary.

Under the Twenty-fifth Dynasty, the length of the unit of measure, the cubit, changed from 44.9 centimeters to 52.4 centimeters, which distinctly modified the proportions established by a reference grid employed for both statuary and reliefs. Nevertheless, the major trend of that period involved a return to the cultural models of the Old and Middle Kingdoms. Both the monarchic ideology of the day and its sculpted expression promoted an orthodoxy of religious practices and styles that yielded remarkably pure forms and high quality execution. Each of the Doukki Gel statues—carved respectively during the half century of the last two reigns of the Twenty-fifth Dynasty and next half century of the first three reigns of the Napatan Dynasty in Upper Nubia (that is to say, between 690 and 593 BCE)—testifies to a particular skill, illustrating the shift from an art strongly influenced by Egyptian workshops to a more African art that slowly adopted its distance from the former.

As already recounted, these seven statues have come down to us in a broken state. Reassembly of the pieces revealed the way they were destroyed, the points of impact, the damaged sections, and the missing fragments. In fact, not many fragments are missing, and apart from one of the statutes of Senkamanisken, whose right hand and left side of face have disappeared, they entail above all chips that must have escaped the attention of the men charged with depositing them in the pit. The blows aimed at the statues were specifically designed to decapitate them, to break the body in two (on occasion), and to hack off arms and legs (or sometimes only feet). The number of fragments varies depending on the size of the statue, the quality of the stone, and the strength of the protagonists. After reassembly, it would appear that the gaps are due either to the loss of certain shards when the statues were brought down, or to their dispersion during the operation. The limited nature of these destructions suggests that the operation was relatively quick, for reasons unknown to us. Here there is no trace of the chiseled obliterations that were so common on depictions of Kushite kings in Egypt at the same period, when the names of a king were erased to deny his existence, the nose was broken to prevent him from breathing, and the double uraeus symbolizing authority over Egypt and Sudan was eliminated to efface this shameful event in Egypt's history. When cartouches or noses are damaged here, it is clear that such damage resulted from the fall of the statue. Only the uraeus on the second statue of Tanutamun seems to have been deliberately smashed.

The oldest, as well as the largest, of these statues depicts Taharqa.

Previous page:
The head of the statue
of Taharqa

Right:
The *mekes* scepter
in Taharqa's right hand

Right:
The head being replaced on
the torso

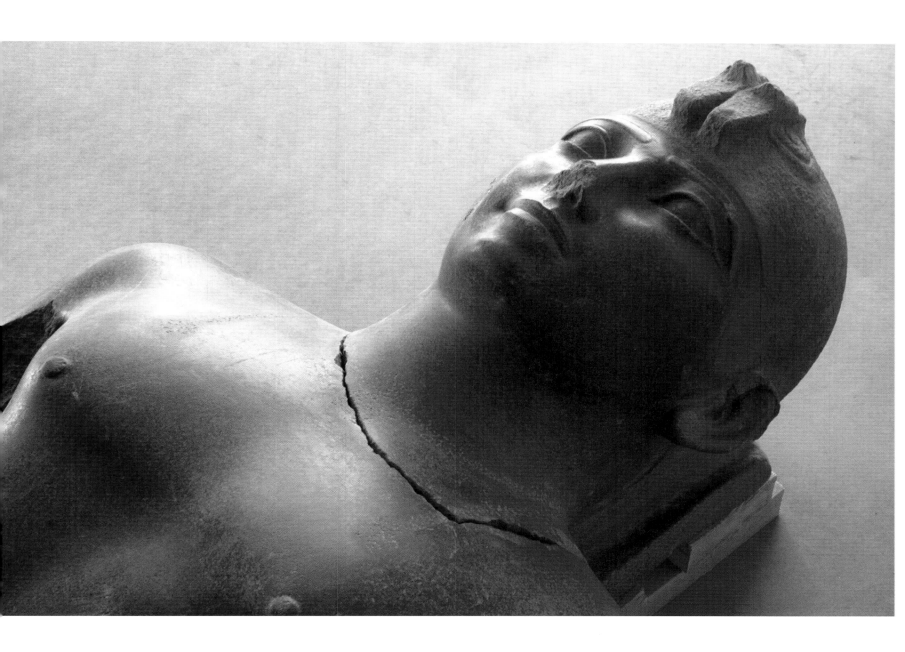

STATUE OF TAHARQA

This statue, carved in a sort of dark gray, fine-grained granite, can be reconstructed from twelve connected fragments: head, torso, right arm (broken into five pieces), right calf, left calf, and the two pieces linking them to the back pillar and base. Only two fragments of the right arm and a piece of the left elbow are missing.

The king's hair is entirely covered by the Kushite skullcap, adorned with the double uraeus in perfect condition. The entire surface of this headdress is stippled, but there is no trace of decoration or lower headband. If either existed, it might have been applied to gilded, fabric-backed plaster, many fragments of which were found in the excavation. The bodies of the cobras, one wearing the white crown, the other wearing the red crown, first form a double bow on the top of the skull and then drop down to the nape of the neck.

The fleshy face displays extremely regular features barely marred by a scar resulting from the fall of the head. The straight, fairly fine nose was slightly chipped on the right side when the statue was beheaded. The lips are full, but not overly so, and they suggest a slight smile. The eyes were given Egyptian-style makeup; the corneas are smooth, and the upper lid is marked by a thin rim. The thick eyelids nearly meet in the middle; the left eyelid is slightly chipped. The ears are somewhat large and well defined. The lobes bear traces of stippling that suggests the application of a golden earring, probably in the form of a ram's head. The powerful neck is almost as wide as the head. The break between head and torso is irregular, and the blow was clearly delivered from behind.

In the current state of the statue, the Kushite neck pendant, usually composed of a cord from which are hung three ram's heads, is also indicated by light stippling, which suggests that, rather than having been obliterated, it was originally depicted in lined, gilded plaster. The largest ram's head, set against the throat, is held by a cord that loops around the neck and falls on either side of the chest, where it ends in two other, smaller ram's heads.

The shoulders are broad and rounded, the chest strong without the muscles being particularly pronounced. The nipples on the breasts are sculpted in relief. The arms,

Taharqa's belt inscribed with his name

Taharqa's Kushite cap-crown
with double uraeus

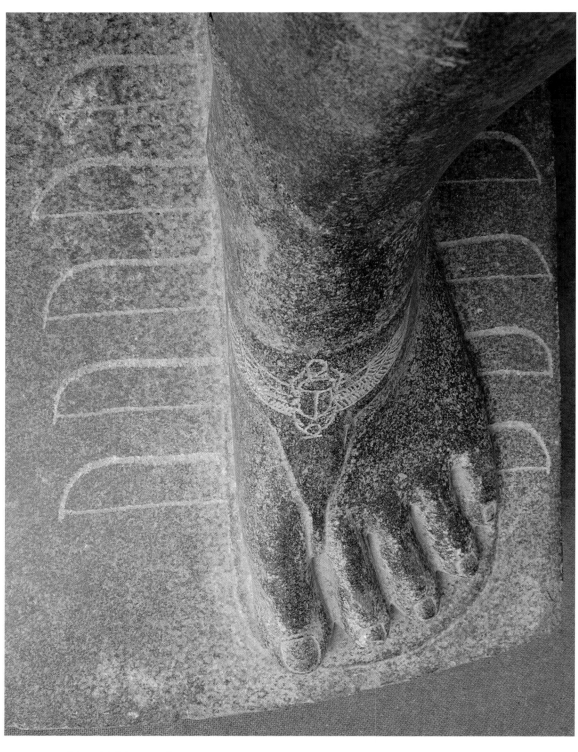

Taharqa's left foot trampling
the Nine Bows

although they are missing several fragments, are strong, and the fists are clenched on a rather short *mekes* scepter. The nail of the extended thumb has been carefully rounded. The narrow hips are draped in a pleated, tight-fitting kilt with a belt bearing the inscription, "The perfect God, Taharqa, living eternally!"

The legs, broken at the knees and ankles, are set solidly on feet that remain fine and elegant despite their size. They are shod in sandals with broad, stippled soles, and the front strap is decorated with a winged scarab whose front legs hold the solar disk while the back legs hold the *shen* sign (representing the orbit of the sun). The toes are spread apart, the nails well defined. The base, which curves slightly in front, bears the representation of the nine foreign lands conquered by Egypt, traditionally symbolized by nine bows engraved under the king's feet (four under the right foot, five under the left).

The upper part of the back pillar is rectangular. It has been slightly battered on the sides and it runs from the middle of the head down to the base. The pillar is distinct at the level of the head, but from the shoulders it begins to merge with the intermediate stone that connects it to the rest of the body. It is engraved with an inscription that gives only the throne name and birth name of the king: "The perfect god, lord of the Two Lands, master of the rites, king of Upper and Lower Egypt Nefertum-Khu-Re, son of Re Taharqa, beloved of Amun-Re who dwells in Pnubs, endowed with all life, stability and power, like Re, eternally." The carving is deep and done with care, revealing special details in the wings of an alighting duck and in the flowering reeds.

Two statues of Taharqa's successor, Tanutamun, were also found in the pit. They are the first free-standing portraits of this king to have been uncovered.

Detail of the winged scarab
decoration on Taharqa's sandal

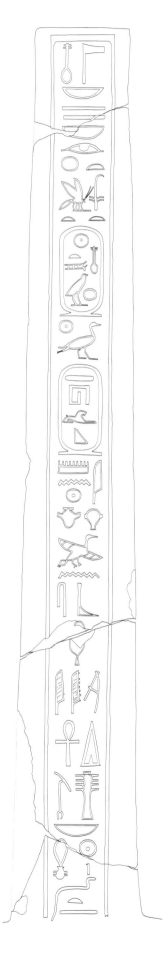

Facsimile of the inscription
on the back pillar of
Taharqa's statue

Dimensions
Height: 218 cm
Height of face: 28 cm
Base: 73.5 x 42.7 x 18 cm
Back pillar: 1.76 cm high
x 22 cm wide (base) and
17 cm wide (top);
5 cm thick behind head

STATUE OF TANUTAMUN (I)

The statue is sculpted in a type of granite that differs from the stone used for Taharqa's portrait. It contains numerous greenish veins and patches, probably mitigated by a thin layer of black paint, some of which can still be seen in places. Today is it composed of seven connected fragments: head, body, three pieces of the left arm, left calf, and the base. It lacks only two small flakes, one between the left arm and the body, the other at the left ankle.

Tanutamun is wearing the same Kushite skullcap as Taharqa, featuring a large double uraeus. The right uraeus, intact, is wearing the white crown, while the red crown on the head of the left uraeus is partly missing. The earlobes display the same stippling seen on Taharqa's statue. The corneas are completely stippled and therefore must have been gilded, whereas the eyelids and eyebrows are understated.

The base with inscription

Right:
Facsimile of the inscription on the back pillar

Following pages:
Head and torso of the statue

Tanutamun's head with cap-crown featuring a very large double uraeus

95

The result is rather striking. The mouth is strangely finer, yet less firm, than Taharqa's.

The fracture between head and body is located just above the neck ornament. The cord has been carved in relief and stippled to receive gilding. The central ram's head is somewhat larger than those dangling on the sides, but the difference is less marked than on Taharqa's neck pendant. The muscles of chest and arms, however, are noticeably more pronounced. The nipples of the breasts are carved in relief. The left arm, although broken into three pieces, is complete. The right arm is intact, and only the front tip of the *mekes* scepter—that powerful symbol of monarchic power—is

broken and flush with the right hand. In addition to the earrings and neck ornament, other jewelry consists of two bracelets represented by stippled bands that are 3.9 centimeters wide.

The belt is inscribed with the king's name: "The perfect God, Tanutamun, endowed with life." The pleats of his kilt are much narrower than those on Taharqa's, even taking into account the difference in size between the two statues.

The left leg is broken under the knee and above the ankle. The stippled soles of the sandals extend beyond the feet, whose toes are spread like those of Taharqa's.

In front of the right foot, the base is carved with an inscription set in a rect-

angle: "The king of Upper and Lower Egypt, lord of the Two Lands Bakare, the son of Re whom he loves Tanutamun, beloved of Amun of Pnubs, endowed with life eternally."

The back pillar is similar to the one on Taharqa's statue. The inscription includes the three names known from other sources, namely Tanutamun's Horus, birth and throne names. "Horus Wahmerut, king of Upper and Lower Egypt Bakare, son of Re Tanutamun, beloved of Amun of Pnubs, endowed with life eternally." The carving is less deep than the hieroglyphs on Taharqa's statute. Therefore, fewer specific paleographic details emerge, but the style is identical.

STATUE OF TANUTAMUN (II)

The statue was carved from a black granite-like stone with red veins that are visible above all on the face and chest. That is probably why it was lightly painted in black, masking the streaks in the rock. It can be reconstructed from fourteen connected fragments: head, chest, six pieces of the left arm, two pieces of the right arm, pelvis, two pieces of the left leg, and the base. The front part of the right hand and the top of the left thigh are missing.

The Kushite skullcap differs from those of the first two statues. The side flaps are proportionally much larger, and the lower edge has a band—indicated by two parallel cords in relief—that passes behind the double uraeus, both in front and back. The two uraei have been deliberately smashed. The earlobes are stippled, whereas the corneas are smooth. The rims of the eyes are more finely drawn than on the first statue of Tanutamun, and the eyebrows are indicated here in low relief. The brows are distinctly wider apart than on Taharqa's statue. The cheekbones are high. The left part of the nose and the chin suffered when the statue was felled, which noticeably alters the facial appearance.

The fracture between head and chest is located in the middle of the neck. The neck ornament is thoroughly similar to the one on the other statue, but the blow to the left shoulder, separating the arm from the torso, damaged the ram's head decorating the left end of the ornament. The muscles of the body are more pronounced here than on the other statue of Tanutamun, whereas the nipples are more discreet. A second break is located above the waist. The pleats of the kilt, from which a large fragment is missing, are similar to those on the other statue. The belt is inscribed with the name of "The perfect God, Tanutamun, endowed with life eter-

nally." The stippled bracelets are 3.7 centimeters wide.

The left leg is broken at the level of the knee, angling down to the middle of the calf, and at the ankle. The right leg is broken above the ankle, making it possible to appreciate the how finely the ankles were rendered. The stippled soles of the sandals extend beyond the feet whose toes are widely separated. The free area in front of the right foot is occupied by an inscription carved within a rectangle: "King of Upper and Lower Egypt, lord of the Two Lands Bakare, son of Re from his belly Tanutamun, beloved [of Amun of P]nubs, endowed with life eternally." The missing hieroglyphs were not deliberately obliterated but damaged when the statue was toppled.

The back pillar is slightly chipped at the top, but its inscription is intact and is identical to the one on the first statue: "Horus Wahmerut, king of Upper and Lower Egypt Bakare, son of Re Tanutamun, beloved of Amun of Pnubs, endowed with life eternally."

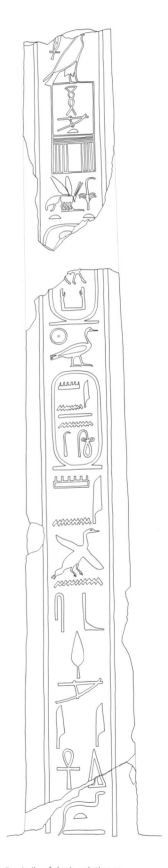

Facsimile of the inscription on the back pillar of the second statue of Tanutamun

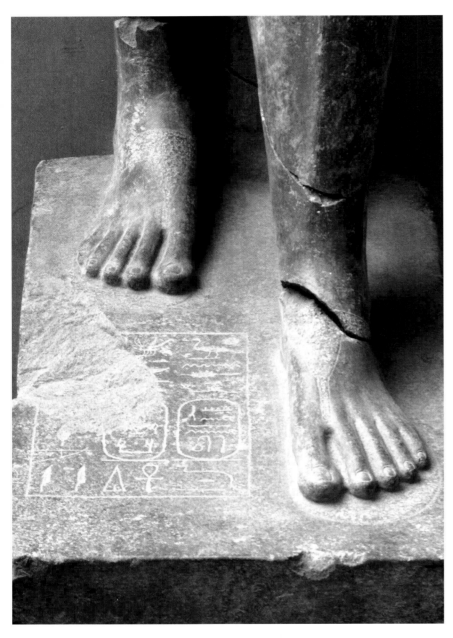

Base of the statue

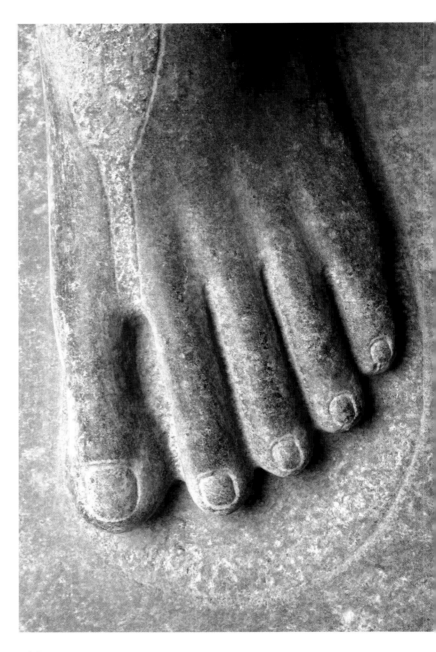

Left foot

Right:
Tanutamun's belt

Ram's head pendant

Dimensions
Height: 197 cm
Height of face: 44 cm
Base: 57 x 32 x 20 cm
Back pillar: 162 cm high
x 17.5 cm wide (base)

The Statues of Senkamanisken, Anlamani, and Aspelta

At the death of Tanutamun, a break between Egypt and Sudan occurred. No statue of the first king of the Napatan Dynasty, Atlanersa, was found in the Doukki Gel pit or in the caches at Gebel Barkal. The two oldest portraits of this new dynasty are therefore the ones of Atlanersa's successor, Senkamanisken.

STATUE OF SENKAMANISKEN (I)

This is probably the only statue carved in real granite. It was broken in nine connected fragments: head, body (which includes a small fragment in the back), two pieces of the right arm, three pieces of the left leg, and the base. Part of the face and the right hand and elbow are missing, as is the sphere that forms the upper part of the headdress.

Although he reigned only over Sudan, the king wears the *pschent*, or double crown linking Upper and Lower Egypt, endowed with a double uraeus. The uraei wear the crowns of Upper and Lower Egypt, respectively, and have remained almost intact despite a blow that disfigured the statue. This must have occurred at the moment of decapitation, delivered from the front at the level of the chin. It is likely that the left half of the face shattered at that moment.

The surviving portion of the face displays very fine carving. The cornea of the sole eye is stippled, as are the earlobes, similar to the first statue of Tanutamun. Since the break between head and body occurred at the level of the chin, that feature suffered greatly.

Tanutamun's head, the left side of which was partly destroyed

103

The neck ornament seems to have been chiseled and stippled slightly below the surface of the skin. The shoulders are wide, the waist narrow. The pronounced and highly realistic muscles of the arms were sculpted from a life model; the arm-bands, bracelets, and anklets are represented by stippled bands that are 2.8, 2.7, and 3 centimeters wide, respectively. The right hand is missing. The kilt is stippled and has no belt; the apron of the kilt is not distinguished from the rest of the cloth.

The long muscles of the legs are deliberately emphasized, like those of the arms. The left leg is broken at the knee and again at the ankle. The tops and the soles of the sandals are stippled. The base of the statue is broken in the lower, front left corner. The base was not inscribed, but it was painted almost to the bottom, which suggests that it was not planted very deep, only four to six centimeters down.

The back pillar takes the form of an obelisk, adapting harmoniously to the back of the headdress. It is inscribed as follows: "Horus Sehertowy, he of the Two Ladies Khahermaat, Golden Horus Userpehty, king of Upper and Lower Egypt Sekheperenre, son of Re Senkamanisken, beloved of Amun of Pnubs." The Horus name, previously known only in the erroneous copy made by Frédéric Cailliaud of the pylon inscriptions—now destroyed—of temple B 700 at Gebel Barkal, is complete on both statues found here. They therefore supply the only complete versions of this monarch's official names. Hence we now dispose of two sure attestations of Senkamanisken's Two Ladies name, Khahermaat, elsewhere incomplete. The hieroglyphs have been carved with elegance, some of them displaying extremely fine details such as the façade of the palace, the rising sun, and the sign for gold.

Dimensions
Height: 155 cm
Height of face: 20 cm
Base: 61 x 30 x 15 cm
Back pillar: 132 cm high
x 17.5 cm wide (base);
the top ends in a
pyramidion

STATUE OF SENKAMANISKEN (II)

The statue was carved from a kind of gray granite somewhat paler than the others; a pink vein runs all the way across the head. It is now composed of five connected fragments: head, chest, pelvis with most of the legs, right forearm, and base. Part of the right hand was broken prior to the destruction of the statue, as shown by traces of gypsum that indicate an ancient attempt at repair.

As in the other statues, the king is depicted in a striding position, the left foot forward, arms falling down his sides. In each hand he holds a *mekes* scepter. Unlike the other statues, however, he is dressed in a *sem* priest's garb, composed of a panther skin draped over the left shoulder with the panther head falling over the front part of the kilt, one paw on the left hip and two others behind, straddling the back pillar.

He is wearing the Kushite skullcap decorated with the double uraeus still complete, wearing both the red crown and the white crown, all stippled to receive gilding. The horizontal band holding the double uraeus is distinguished from the cap by a slight ridge at the top. The modeling of the face is subtle and the almond-shaped eyes are well defined—even the tear ducts are visible. The corneas are entirely stippled. The mouth and nose are particularly fine. The head was separated from the body at the level of the neck ornament and a fragment of neck, on the right, was lost during demolition. The central and right-hand pendants of the neck ornament seem to have been chiseled off, unless they were stippled in slight intaglio in order to receive appliquéd features. Other jewelry is indicated by stippled bands for armbands, bracelets, and anklets. The kilt is handled in a schematic, completely stippled manner that makes an effective contrast with the

Frontal view
of Senkamanisken's face

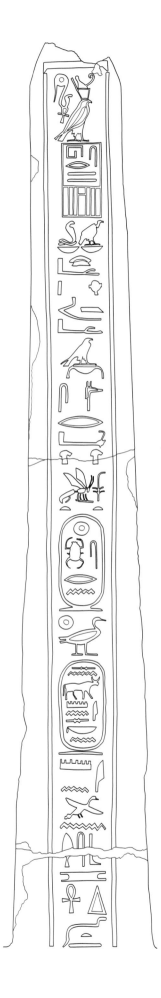

black-painted skin even without the gold leaf that must have adorned it.

The legs were broken above the ankles. The feet are shod with stippled sandals and stand on a rectangular base that bears the following inscription: "King of Upper and Lower Egypt, lord of the Two Lands, [Senkamani]sken beloved of Amun of Pnubs, endowed with life, like Re, eternally." The upper part of the cartouche was crushed in the pit by the bust of one of the statues of Tanutamun. It was therefore not

deliberately obliterated. The back pillar is obelisk-shaped, like the other statue of Senkamanisken, but the pyramidion ends at the nape of the neck. It is inscribed as follows: "Horus Sehertowy, he of the Two Ladies Khahermaat, Golden Horus Userpehty, king of Upper and Lower Egypt Sekheperenre, son of Re Senkamanisken, beloved of Amun of Pnubs, endowed with life eternally." The hieroglyphs are noticeably less detailed than on the other statue of Senkamanisken.

Panther head overlapping
the waist of the kilt

Right:
Facsimile of the inscription on
the back pillar

Far right:
Rear view of the second statue
of Senkamanisken

STATUE OF ANLAMANI

Carved in a kind of dark gray granite, this statue was broken into only six connected fragments: head (to which should be added a small piece of the right uraeus), body, two shards from the tip of the right-hand *mekes*, and base. The left arm is missing. The smooth parts of the statue were less finely polished than their Twenty-fifth Dynasty counterparts, and were painted black.

The king is crowned with the *pschent*, adorned with a pair of ram's horns. The ball at the top of the crown is missing. The two uraei, slightly chipped, wear the white and red crown, respectively. A fragment from the head of the right uraeus was put back in place. The crown, horns, and double uraeus are all stippled. This is the only known example of a royal statue with the horns of Amun, although these appear in painted portraits of the heads of Egyptian monarchs on the walls of Theban tombs starting with the reign of Thutmose III. The face was modeled with care. The slightly slanting eyes were lightly stippled yet were painted. The rims of the lids were delicately stressed in relief. The cheekbones are high, the nostrils and lips are broad. The head was separated from the body just above the neck ornament, which seems to have been chiseled off.

The torso is fairly similar to that of the earlier statues. The arms are held back along the sides, with armbands at the tops and bracelets at the wrists, in the form of stippled bands measuring 2.8 and 2.2 centimeters, respectively. The front parts of the *mekes* scepters are broken.

The rendering of the kilt has been simplified—there are no pleats. The boundary between the fabric and the right leg is barely visible in raking light; the same is true of the layered fabrics under the belt.

Dimensions
Height: 178 cm
Height of face: 37 cm
(remaining, with crown)
Height of horns: 13 cm
Base: 59.5 x 28 x 15 cm
Back pillar: 165 cm high
x 17 cm wide (base);
the top ends in a
pyramidion

Far left:
The top of the restored
statue of Anlamani
with Aspelta in the
background

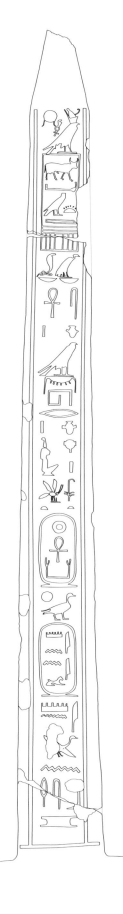

The belt bears an engraved inscription, painted in yellow: "The perfect god Anlamani, endowed with life." The legs and arms are muscled, the ankles adorned with anklets in the form of stippled bands 2.5 centimeters wide. The feet, shod in stippled sandals, are fine, the toes are slightly splayed. The soles are suggested only by light stippling on the base. The front of the base is curved and wider at the top, most likely designed to fit into a special cavity in the ground. In front of the right foot there seems to be an incomplete inscription of royal names.

The back pillar takes the form of a slender obelisk that is well adapted to the back of the *pschent*. The tip of the obelisk, like that of the crown, is missing. The inscription was not engraved as deeply as on the three other Napatan statues. "Horus the victorious bull Khaemmaat, he of the Two Ladies Seankhib, Golden Horus Heryibhermaat, king of Upper and Lower Egypt Ankhare, son of Re Anlamani, beloved of Amun of Pnubs." Interestingly, the Two Ladies name is given here as Seankhib, whereas it is rendered elsewhere as Sankhibtowy or Seankhtowy. The Golden Horus name, meanwhile, is given in full here—Heryibhermaat—whereas it appears only in abbreviated forms on Anlamani's other preserved monuments as either Heryhermaat or Heryibmaat.

Far left:
The head of Anlamani with *pschent* crown and horns of Amun

Left:
Facsimile of inscription on the back pillar

Right:
Rear view of the statue of Anlamani

Dimensions
Height: 123 cm
Height of face: 18.5 cm
Base: 40 x 22 x 11 cm
Back pillar: 9.6 cm thick
x 10.5 cm wide (top) and
13.5 cm thick x 28 cm
wide (bottom)

STATUE OF ASPELTA

The statue was carved in a kind of plain gray granite, and is now composed of four connected fragments: head, body, legs, and base. The left leg has been almost entirely destroyed below the knee. The statue is covered with a thin film of black paint. The king is wearing the Kushite skullcap adorned with the double uraeus, on which both white and red crowns are intact. A fragment of gilded plaster is still in place on the top of the head. The face is round; the eyes are almond-shaped with stippled corneas. The tip of the rather short nose was damaged when the head toppled. The well-defined mouth harbors a smile. The break between head and body occurs in the middle of the neck. The ram's head pendants on the neck ornament have been visibly chiseled.

The modeling of the body and the handling of the kilt are similar to that found on the second statue of Senkamanisken. Red lines indicating corrections can still be seen around the edges of the kilt—perhaps they should be interpreted as a sign of incompletion even though the statue was already painted black. The polish of the skin areas is noticeably less fine, similar to the polish on the statue of Anlamani.

The legs are broken below the knee and at the ankle. The rendering of the feet seems a little less refined in comparison to previous statues, but the smaller dimensions of this work and the poor quality of the stone should be taken into account. The stippling of the sandals merges with the grainy appearance of the adjacent skin. The front of the base is slightly curved. An inscription is lightly engraved, at a slight angle, in front of the right foot: "Perfect god Merykare, lord of the Two Lands Aspelta, beloved of Amun of Pnubs."

The top of the back pillar is rectangular, but the sides are slightly battered. The

Aspelta's ram-head neck ornament, chiseled flat

Head of Aspelta, left profile

Right:
Facsimile of inscription on back pillar

Far right:
Rear view of the statue of Aspelta

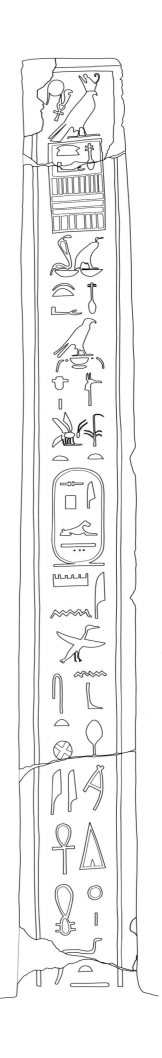

inscription on the pillar is much more meticulous than the one on the base: "Horus Neferkha, he of the Two Ladies Neferkha, Golden Horus Userib, king of Upper and Lower Egypt Aspelta, beloved of Amun of Pnubs, endowed with life, like Re, eternally."

Egyptian Sculptors in Nubia

Apart from a very few exceptions, it is generally the rule that we lack a sufficient number of sculptures—even in Egypt, where they are legion—to determine the stylistic features of the workshops that produced them. Nevertheless, in certain instances criteria specific to a given milieu or region have been established. Large royal statues were executed in workshops answering directly to the king who might assign one of his artists, as a particular favor, to another monarch or to a high civil servant he wanted to honor. Usually, however, the artists appointed to serve the pharaoh worked in the palace workshop or on one of the kingdom's various construction sites. Autobiographies of construction overseers and archives from the royal tombs give us a good idea of the organization of major building projects. One of the stela that Taharqa erected in the temple at Kawa records the arrival of artists from Memphis to redo the temple. Thus several iconographic themes seen on the walls of the mortuary temples of kings from the Fifth and Sixth Dynasties, Sahure, Nyuserre, and Pepy II, can also be seen in first court of the Kawa temple, such as the king as a sphinx trampling his enemies underfoot.

Although no extant texts corroborate the arrival at Kerma of an Egyptian sculptor—

or Egyptian-trained sculptor—summoned to execute the statue of Taharqa, the style of the Egyptian school is clear. The inscription on the back pillar, stating that the king was "beloved of Amun-Re who dwells in Pnubs," suggests that the sculpture was done on the spot, and the stone in which it was carved probably came from quarries located at the third cataract, some twenty kilometers away. There are few surviving sculptures of the king, however, that allow us to carry out precise comparative analysis. The heads of several of his colossal statues have disappeared, and available reproductions of those that survive do not permit the kind of examination required for this type of analysis; the other heads or complete statues that have survived are small in scale or cast in

bronze. Furthermore, the provenance of those works is rarely known. Finally, while some statues lack heads, some bodiless heads lack inscriptions that make positive identification possible.

Among the fifteen or so stone statues of Taharqa known to exist, only two heads are suitable for comparison: the colossus at Gebel Barkal (now at the Sudan National Museum, Khartoum) and a head in the Egyptian Museum in Cairo, alleged to come from temple of Karnak near Thebes. The latter has benefited from fine reproductions in books on art, whereas the former has not received the attention it deserves. On both statues, the king is shown wearing the crown of Onuris. (In the myth of the Distant Goddess the sun god Re sends Onuris, in the form of Shu,

Left:
Frontal view of Taharqa's head

Top:
Left profile of Taharqa

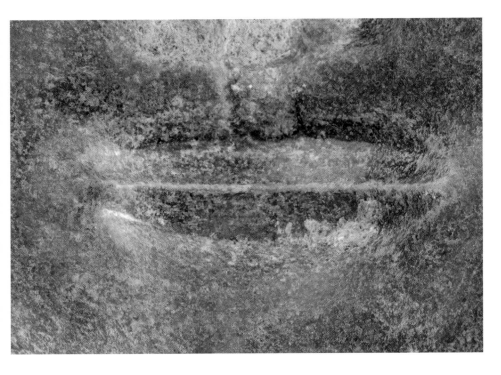

Top:
Taharqa's left eye, detail

Bottom:
Taharqa's mouth, detail

into Nubia to seek after the god's daughter, a lioness known for her cruelty. Onuris manages to tame the goddess and turn her into a cat.) The crown is composed of four tall plumes attached at the back to a cylindrical base (*modius*) placed on top of the Kushite cap to form a single headdress. It should nevertheless be noted that on these two statues, the Kushite cap displays a feature not found on the Doukki Gel statue or on other contemporaneous statues or reliefs: the two side flaps in front of the ears seem to be made of a thick fabric edged with a hem. Whereas the double uraeus and the upper part of the crown have vanished from the Karnak head, they partially survived on the Gebel Barkal colossus, which stands at 4.18 meters. Damage to both statues, however, gives them a special appearance. The Gebel Barkal colossus is the larger of the two. To judge from published reproductions, the styles of the three statues are quite different, though all three are of fine quality. The same basic facial features recur on the three portraits: a fleshy face with finely rimmed, almond-shaped eyes topped by thick eyebrows brought quite close together, and a well-defined mouth, full but not excessively so. The nose is refined, but extant only on the Doukki Gel statue. The ears are large, yet proportional to the face. The three portraits nevertheless render the king's handsomeness differently. The two sculptures found in Nubia render him as a very young man, whereas the Karnak statue, with more heavily etched features, more prominent cheekbones, and thicker lips, gives the king an older appearance. These differences might be a chronological marker but might also represent distinct stylistic trends.

Without appropriate photographs or adequate lighting, it is hard to make detailed observations of the Gebel Barkal colossus currently on display in the entrance of the Sudan National Museum,

Taharqa's head, right profile

Khartoum. When it comes to the Doukki Gel statue, however, we might wonder to what extent the sculptor was conforming to a school that glorified the monarch's perfection, rather than stressing particular facial features. In other words, the artist might have had links with a Memphis workshop, whereas the sculptor of the statue now in Cairo would have represented the Theban School. The absence of contemporaneous royal statuary from the north, however, obliges us to induce its specificities from earlier or later works. Whereas five fragmentary monumental statues of Taharqa by the Thebes school have survived, only one headless torso of the king was found at Tanis and no Memphis sculpture of him has surfaced to date. Meanwhile, the two statues carried off by Esarhaddon during the Assyrian conquest of Taharqa's kingdom in 671—the bases of which were found in the palace of Tell Nebi Unis in Iraq—could have been taken from anywhere in Egypt.

Stylistic analysis of a statue cannot rest upon the head alone. Distinct differences can be noted between the Doukki Gel statue and the Gebel Barkal colossus, the

latter appearing heavier and more schematic, as seen in the shape of the somewhat fatter neck and the slightly protruding shoulder blades on the torso. No trace of jewelry can be seen on the available photographs of the colossus, no neck ornament, bracelet, or anklet. It is nevertheless striking that the hips, ringed by a belt engraved with the king's name, are absolutely identical in both statues; the handling of the kilt is very similar and the muscles of the legs are clearly marked, as also seen on contemporaneous stelae and reliefs. The feet, shod in simple sandals that are stippled but without any special decoration, trample the Nine Bows engraved on the rectangular base, as on the Doukki Gel statue.

Finally there is the statue of Taharqa as a sphinx, originally from Kawa and now in the British Museum, plus the statuettes in front of the rams at the Kawa temple, and the 1,070 *shabti* figures placed in his tomb at Nuri. Although the statuettes were placed in front of and inside the Kawa temple, it is safe to assume that they were done by local artists. The sphinx is an original creation, in comparison to the Egyptian human-headed sphinxes of the Middle Kingdom or even those of the New Kingdom. Nevertheless, the leonine enlargement of the features that makes Taharqa's face unrecognizable can also be seen on many other sphinxes, such as those from the Middle Kingdom or even the Hatshepsut sphinx now in the Metropolitan Museum of New York. As to the statuettes associated with the rams, they rarely resemble their royal model. When it comes to the *shabtis* (funerary figures designed to perform chores for the deceased in the afterlife,) it is interesting to note that although they display a family resemblance there are marked differences from one figure to the next, and though some of the larger ones are quite big—up to sixty centimeters tall—their features remain schematic. The African features on most of the figures are obviously striking, for such features are not found on the three statues discussed above. Here again, it is difficult to decide discern whether this difference stems king's age when the statue was sculpted, or if it reflects an underlying ideology.

The problems posed by the statue of Taharqa recur with the statues of Tanutamun. This time, however, comparison must be limited to the two Doukki Gel examples, since the other two sculpted portraits of the king, found in Gebel Barkal, are headless. Prior to the Doukki Gel discovery, the only image of Tanutamun's face was that gleaned by studying the painted profile in his tomb at al-Kurru and the relief carving in the Osiris–Ptah–Lord of Life chapel in Karnak, where depictions of the king alternate with that of his predecessor, Taharqa. It has also been supposed that the small head of Amun found at Sanam, which bore the beginning of his titulary, was carved in Tanutamun's image; otherwise we had to be content with the top of a canopic jar and the rather simple *shabtis* of the king from his tomb.

The surviving reliefs and paintings suggest that Tanutamun was, like his predecessor, a very handsome man. In the Osiris–Ptah–Lord of Life chapel, he is sometimes shown wearing the Kushite headdress, sometimes with the red crown or the white crown. The deeply and carefully carved reliefs at Karnak are typical of the style of the Twenty-fifth Dynasty, whereas the more schematic paintings in the royal tomb convey the purity of his features but create an impression of timeless unreality. Although it is often tricky to identify depictions of the same subject done in two and in three dimensions, the surviving reliefs are obviously individualized, as confirmed by comparison of

Far left:
Torso and thighs of Taharqa

Left:
Right profile of Tanutamun's head, first statue

Right profile of Tanutamun carved in relief in the chapel of Osiris-Ptah-Lord of Life, Karnak

Following pages:
Frontal view of the head of Tanutamun, first statue

Frontal view of the head of Tanutamun, second statue

123

portraits of Taharqa and Tanutamun in the same chapel. Juxtaposition of these profiles with the first statue of Tanutamun is evocative, and the resemblance is indisputable. The nose is straight but slightly rounded at the tip, the lips are full but not fat, and the chin is well defined.

At first sight the two statues of Tanutamun recovered from the pit at Doukki Gel are very different from one another. Although the facial features are similar and perfectly recognizable (ignoring the damage done to the chin of the second statue), much of the difference stems from the modeling. On the face of the first statue the eyebrows, rims of the eyelids, and lips are not underscored by a fine incision, as they are on the second. These two stylistic options co-existed throughout the history of Egyptian portraiture, both royal and private. The corneas of the eyes are entirely stippled to receive gilding on the first, but are smooth on the second, which considerably alters the expression. Finally, the Kushite skullcap, stippled on both statues, features merely the large double uraeus on the first statue (when seen from the front), whereas the second also has a double bulge that marks the band that held the uraei to the king's head. If we compare the style of these sculptures to the style of Taharqa's portraits, we see that the technique used for the second statue of Tanutamun is relatively similar to the statue of Taharqa found at Doukki Gel and, indeed, to that of Thebes. When it comes to examples similar to the first statue of Tanutamun, we have to look elsewhere.

Whereas the statue of Taharqa was striking in its total perfection, the first statue of Tanutamun is surprising for an equally remarkable style that, in theory, belongs to neither the Egyptian nor the Kushite canons. Whereas the cheekbones are more marked on the first statue, the muscles of the body are generally less pronounced in comparison to the second statue. But the above-mentioned characteristics—namely the absence of incisions underscoring eyes and mouth, the stippling of corneas—and above all the unusual height of the upright cobras and the finely carved relief of their fanned necks, give this work a startlingly Far-Eastern feel. There is obviously no question of seeking such influences, however—the beholder's impression stems from the coincidence of several combined factors not found elsewhere. Egyptian images of cobras, for instance, commonly stressed this impressive feature of the upright serpent, as seen not only on painted silhouettes of Tanutamun in his tomb, but even on a statuette of Psamtik II.

Mention has often been made here of the way Twenty-fifth Dynasty artists referred to royal sculpture of the Old and Middle Kingdoms. Resemblances are particularly striking in the modeling of the bodies of the statues of Taharqa and Tanutamun. Among the statues, however, there is a greater or lesser emphasis on the muscles of the torso, arms, and legs. In all three cases we are dealing with young bodies with strong muscles, though the musculature is not emphasized as strongly as it is in contemporaneous bas-reliefs. The same is generally true of the statues found at Gebel Barkal. The belts are engraved in fairly similar fashion, the main difference being the wishful invocation that follows the king's name. The kilts are very similar, though Tanutamun's pleats are tighter than Taharqa's. The carving of the feet is very meticulous on all three statues, but only Taharqa's sandals are adorned with a decorative scarab etched onto the front strap.

Several influences therefore weighed upon the conception of these statues. The artists were probably Egyptian and—without regard to their assumed membership in a specific school—they followed the general trends of the day: the imitation of the ancient statues still visible in certain temples at the time; a concern to respect highly orthodox artistic tradition; and use of a few specifically Twenty-fifth Dynasty features such as full faces. This inspiration, drawn from Old and Middle Kingdom sources, itself contains a certain ambivalence in so far as each of those two periods had its own specificities that give rise to contradictions if one tries to combine them in a single work. Thus the timeless aspect that tended to characterize Old Kingdom art—that Egyptians held so dear precisely because it perfectly conveyed their aspiration for eternal life—was sometimes offset by the capacity of Middle Kingdom portraits to convey a good idea of the subject's personality. Both styles can be identified, sometimes intermingled, in Kushite statuary, reflecting an aptitude for the skillful reproduction of an individual's features yet ultimately idealized. The statues of Tanutamun illustrate each of those tendencies in turn. It is also worth stressing that the first statue of Tanutamun displays all the characteristics that would later be found on statues of the early Napatan Period.

Kushite Artists of Egyptian Inspiration

Largely due to a dearth of material, we still lack some important information needed for an analysis of Kushite sculpture, notably the identification of the workshops where sculptors trained. Nevertheless, certain parameters can be established by examining the statues of the first monarchs of the young Napatan Dynasty. The weight of the Egyptian model remained significant, but the originality of the new royal workshops can be clearly detected.

No portrait of Atlanersa has turned up in any of the caches at Gebel Barkal and Doukki Gel, nor anywhere else, for that matter, despite the fact that several temples and major buildings erected by that king survive. In contrast, the two statues of Senkamanisken discovered at Doukki Gel allow us to compare quite different works, as we did with those of Tanutamun. In Senkamanisken's case we can also refer to three statues from Gebel Barkal—one complete and two headless, one of which is dressed in a panther skin—plus a statue of his wife, Amanimalel. Both sets of statues, then, included a portrait of the Kushite king dressed as a *sem* priest, something not very common in Egypt where there are nevertheless many liturgical depictions of the monarch in finery associated with the various ceremonies over which he presided. Such statues, furthermore, were usually small in size, designed to be carried in official processions. Here both statues are nearly human size and thus belong to the category of monumental sculpture. A human-headed sphinx of the king, placed in the first court of the grand temple of Amun at Napata (now in the Sudan National Museum, Khartoum), along with the 1,277 *shabtis* buried in his tomb at

Nuri, offer additional comparative material, as do various fragmentary monuments.

It is unfortunate that the left side of Senkamanisken's face on the first statue at Doukki Gel is missing, in so far as the modeling here seems to be superior to that on the second statue. The influence of Egyptian sculpture is also still quite evident. This face, although different from all the others, is comparable to the one on the first statue of Tanutamun in terms of the subtlety of the features, the decision not to underscore eyebrows or eyelids, and the stippling of corneas to prepare for the gilding of the eyes. The head of the second statue has the same characteristics but, despite indisputably masterful execution, it belongs to an original culture stylistically distinct from northern models. The Kushite skullcap is treated in a new way, with a rather narrow headband holding the double uraeus.

Even the panther skin worn by the *sem* priest, borrowed from the Egyptian repertoire, indicates a shift toward specific local practices. The schematic handling of the kilt on the first statue is another stylistic feature of this school of sculptors. The overall pose of the two statues is identical, of course, but we are in the presence of a different art that steadily asserted itself during a single reign, and then went on to pursue its own development in subsequent reigns. The complete statue of Senkamanisken found at Gebel Barkal (now in the Boston Museum of Fine Arts), and the human-headed sphinx from temple B 500 display a rougher style with less subtle modeling. Senkamanisken's *shabtis*, meanwhile, like those made for Taharqa, were executed in stone or glaze by less skillful craftsmen and would not be iden-

tifiable if the king's name were not engraved on them, even though some of the figures in serpentine are veritable statues with individualized features.

The face of Senkamanisken's successor, Anlamani, is known not just from the Doukki Gel statue but also from two statues found in the Gebel Barkal cache, as well as from the *shabtis* in his tomb. One of the two Gebel Barkal statues is a colossus nearly four meters tall, wearing the Onuris crown; the other is a life-size statue whose face is recognizable despite damage to the nose and mouth that it likely incurred when it fell. The Doukki Gel statue, however, is peerless: here we have a unique masterpiece, executed according to the same stylistic criteria employed for the first statue of Tanutamun and the two statues of Senkamanisken. Whereas the fleshy faces on the Gebel Barkal statues seem somewhat stereotyped, the one on the Doukki Gel example is much more subtle and individualized, and perhaps younger. It is also enhanced by its extraordinary headdress, a *pschent* adorned with a double uraeus and the two horns of Amun. It is the sole extant three-dimensional royal portrait with this feature on the head to be found in either Egypt or Sudan. The horns spring from the king's temples and ring his ears in a particularly harmonious way, whether viewed from the front or the side. The only sculpture with these attributes that comes to mind is a more recent statue of a human-headed Amun (now in the Egyptian Museum, Cairo). The horns spring from the *modius* in the same way, but the limestone sculp-

The head of Anlamani

128

Head of the first statue of
Senkamanisken

Head of the second statue of
Senkamanisken

ture is quite damaged, making it hard to appreciate the overall design. Finally, it is worth pointing out the body of Anlamani is much more svelte here than in the Gebel Barkal statues.

The last statue in the Doukki Gel cache, depicting Aspelta, is also the smallest of the seven. Here again, we see that the king is shown as very young, probably even younger than the colossus found in fragments in the Gebel Barkal caches, despite the strong resemblance. Aspelta's colossus, like those of Taharqa and Anlamani, was given the lofty Onuris crown, and measured 3.32 meters; his eyebrows, eyelids, and lips are conspicuously underscored, like those of Taharqa's colossus but unlike the other portrait statues at Gebel Barkal. The face of Aspelta on the statue found in Doukki Gel, meanwhile, imitates the same stylistic criteria seen on the first statue of Tanutamun and those of Senkamanisken and Anlamani. The band holding the double uraeus is rendered not unlike the one on the second statue of Senkamanisken, although more of the forehead shows. The highly meticulous modeling of the body is more individualized here than on other examples. Other three-dimensional portraits of Anlamani include a sphinx found at Defeia, near Khartoum, whose sculpted surface has degraded significantly, and nearly three hundred more or less complete *shabtis*, which were part of his tomb furnishings.

Following these meager comparisons, reign by reign, of the very few significant surviving examples of contemporaneous statuary, we will now attempt to describe the specificities that emerge from the seven statues found at Doukki Gel, in the context of previous knowledge in this area. Art historians and Nubian specialists have often stressed the difficulty of dealing with this sculpture and its development between the eighth and sixth centuries BCE given the extremely limited number of items available

for study. The Doukki Gel discovery therefore represents a significant contribution to the pivotal period when the Napatan kingdom progressively moved away from the artistic influence it had sought in Egypt. The state of existing documentation, even when published, hardly facilitates detailed comparisons. Nevertheless, observations we have made on the statues are sometimes echoed in more or less precise written descriptions found in specialized literature.

As for headdress, five of our seven statues wear the Kushite skullcap, with significant differences in the size, shape, and position of the band designed to hold the double uraeus. Taharqa's skullcap descends low on his brow, has no band, and seems to cling to his head almost too tightly. This particular feature recurs on the colossus from Gebel Barkal and the head found at Thebes; in fact, the tight fit corresponds to the needs of the heavy Onuris headdress rather than the simple Kushite skullcap itself. The first statue of Tanutamun also wears a fairly tight skullcap, but one that is shorter and reveals more forehead, lending the headwear a different appearance. Finally, the skullcaps on the second statue of Senkamanisken and that of Aspelta both have wide bands. The same model can be seen on one of the Senkamanisken statues found at Gebel Barkal.

Strangely, the *pschent* is depicted twice, on Anlamani and on the second statue of Senkamanisken, that is *after* the divorce between the Egyptian and Napatan kingdoms. Finally, the Amun horns that spring from the red crown worn by Anlamani are an extremely important addition. As mentioned above, the horns are attested on various headdresses worn by Egyptian pharaohs since the reign of Thutmose III, and they were clearly linked to the divine nature of the king and his cult image, notably during the reign of Amenhotep III in the temple of the royal *ka* at Luxor and

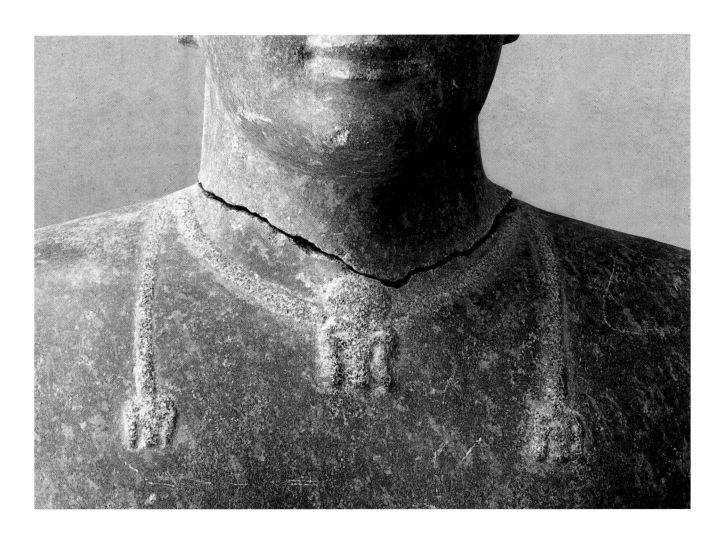

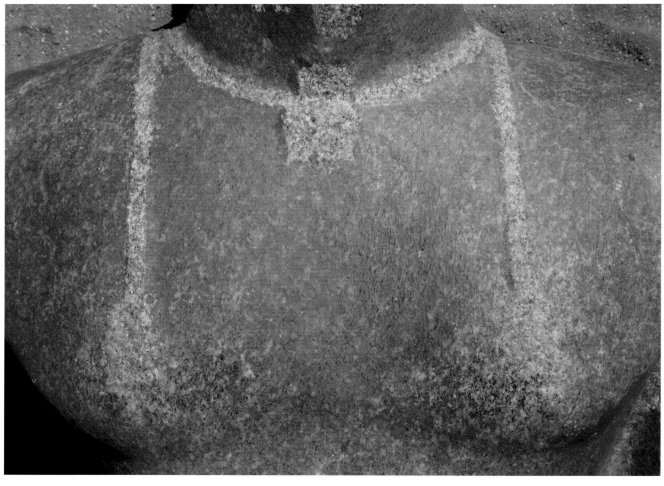

Top:
Neck ornament with ram's-head
pendants on first statue of Tanutamun

Bottom:
Neck ornament on first statue of
Senkamanisken, chiseled away

his jubilee temple in Soleb. Depiction of Amun's horns perhaps became more common on Napatan and Meroitic reliefs, but only a fuller, systematic study of the divine attribute in this context will provide more complete answers.

When it comes to regalia, the *mekes* scepter is consistently found in the hands of these kings, whoever they may be. It was a strong monarchic symbol because it contained the papyrus scroll bearing the *imyt-per,* the title of the king's ownership of Egypt; at Doukki Gel it was unfailingly included, as it was on the statues of Gebel Barkal. This one Egyptian model was therefore repeated relentlessly, whereas Egyptian royal statues of all periods were endowed with a much more varied range of attributes. The same could be said of the kilt, or *shendjyt,* showed in pleated form on the late Twenty-fifth Dynasty statues and in a more schematic way on the others, except for the colossus of Anlamani at Gebel Barkal where the sculptor rendered the pleats with great care. Senkamanisken is the only king to wear a panther skin, seen on one of his statues at Doukki Gel and another at Gebel Barkal. Egyptian iconography did not usually show kings wearing this garment—in theory, it designated either the function of the *sem* priest or Iunmutef, therefore more suited to the king's eldest son or his deputy, notably in the role of funerary priest officiating in the rites for the deceased monarch. The use of the garment in Napatan and Meroitic contexts remains to be fully explained. Aspelta can be seen wearing it on the walls of the hypostyle hall of temple T at Kawa in the context of classic scenes of offerings.

The jewelry, on the other hand, has been the object of specific research, notably the neck ornament comprising a cord and ram's head pendant presented frontally, with two more frontal ram's heads dangling from the ends of the cord on either side of the chest. This pendant is present on all the statues at Doukki Gel, on most of those found at Gebel Barkal, and on the two headless torsos of Taharqa found at Karnak-North and now at the Egyptian Museum in Cairo. Yet it appears to be absent from the colossus of Taharqa at Gebel Barkal; on the Napatan statues at Doukki Gel it has merely been stippled into the surface in order to receive gilding, like the bracelets. Only bracelets figure on the statues of Taharqa and Tanutamun, whereas the Napatan kings also wear armbands and anklets. We have already mentioned the traces of stippling on the earlobes of Taharqa and Tanutamun that must have received earrings of gilded stucco; it is likely they also featured the motif of the frontal ram's head, as seen on reliefs of a chapel erected by Shebitqo at Karnak.

Examination of the surface of these statues reveals an almost perfect polish in the case of Taharqa, becoming less and less perfect from reign to reign. The stone used for the portrait of Taharqa is very dark. The first statue of Tanutamun contains dark green veins, the second pink veins, which must have been attenuated by a thin layer of paint that is hard to discern today. In contrast, the traces of paint on the Napatan statues are unmistakable. A black coat covers the natural gray color of the rock, while visible traces of red lines reflect either a specific stage of execution or a polychrome state. The gilding that must have been applied to the stippled parts of the statues—either directly or with a plastered fabric support—covered all of the crowns, the eyes of the first statue of Tanutamun and those of all the Napatan statues, the jewelry, the kilts of the Napatan statues, the panther skin of the second statue of Senkamanisken, and the sandals on all statues.

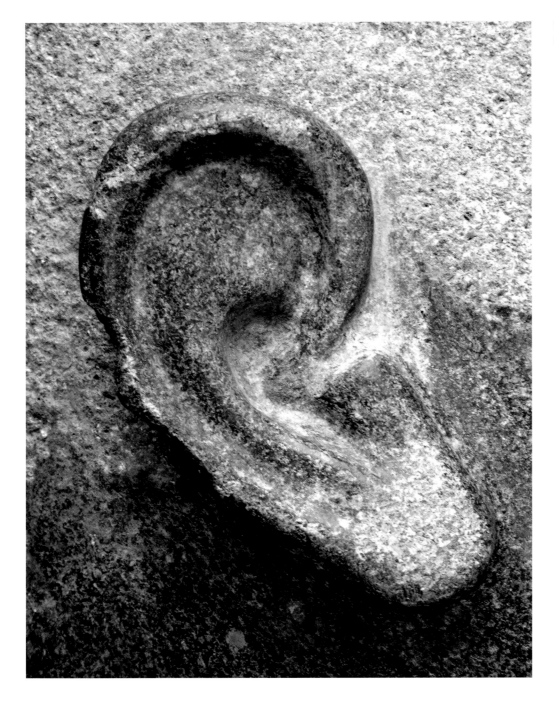

Stippling on right earlobe, statue of Taharqa

Before their destruction, these statues had enjoyed long lives—nearly a century in the case of Taharqa. They had therefore been carefully maintained; also, they bear various signs of alterations of their presentation. Thus certain neck ornaments that were initially sculpted seem to have been chiseled off, probably to better receive the gilded stucco that would stand out so well against the black skin. Traces of oil or unguents remain on the body of Taharqa and on the backs of certain leaves of gold. The restorer has therefore suggested that the statue might have been entirely gilded at some point. Meanwhile, traces of red and yellow paint are visible on certain parts of the sculptures. We might thus speculate whether the *pschent* on the first statue of Senkamanisken was painted at one point in time and gilded at another.

Statue of Akhratan
(Museum of Fine Arts, Boston)

Yellow ocher, visible in the hieroglyphs on Anlamani's belt, was used to enhance the gold color. Finally, it should be noted that there were rather clumsy attempts to restore the right hand of the second statue of Senkamanisken and the left hand of the statue of Aspelta.

It is hard to know to what extent the few surviving Napatan statues from reigns that followed Aspelta's should be considered as representative of that period. One of them, headless, originally from the region of Napata, is now in the Aegyptisches Museum in Berlin. It shows Aspelta's successor, Aramatelqo, seated, wearing a jubilee cloak and holding the scepter and flail, clearly mimicking an Egyptian sculpture from the Old or Middle Kingdom. The only other royal statue accurately attributable to a king of this lineage shows Akhratan in a striding pose. The sculptor, unable to study the broken colossi buried in the caches, clearly turned for inspiration to the small statue of Amenhotep III that Piankhy had transferred from Soleb to Gebel Barkal, as revealed by his handling of the kilt and the wavy motif on the belt. This statue, like the one that inspired it, was barely 1.30 meters tall when it was still intact.

Three other comparisons merit discussion. The first is the unfinished colossus found at Tumbus, whose pleated kilt suggests a last attempt to Egyptianize an art that was moving further and further away from its original stylistic sources. There is also a large anonymous statue, found nearly intact in Atlanersa's temple B 700 at Gebel Barkal, is unique in style though influenced by Egyptian technique and therefore very hard to date; somewhat more massive than Twenty-fifth Dynasty statues, it is nevertheless of very fine quality. The face is round but the features are fairly refined, and the king was crowned with the *pschent* adorned with a double

uraeus. The modeling of the fleshy chest is quite striking. Finally, the truly massive colossi of Tabo already belong to another era. Although endowed with Egyptian features of double crown, false beard, and two *mekes* scepters, they display a certain number of new characteristics. Their features have a heaviness previously seen only on Napatan sphinxes, the *pschent* is ringed with a wreath of laurel leaves, and kings are dressed in both a kind of tunic with suspenders knotted at the shoulder and a kilt of the *shendjyt* type affixed by a belt knotted in front. The wide pleats of the kilt are more reminiscent of a Roman soldier's tunic than of a pharaonic garment.

One of the colossi from Tabo (Sudan National Museum, Khartoum)

The colossus at Tumbus lying in
the quarry where it was carved

A TUMULTUOUS HISTORY

In order to understand the circumstances in which these statues were first installed in the temple of Amun of Pnubs, and then subsequently toppled and buried, it is important to discuss what we know of the lives and reigns of these five kings within the context of historical events in Egypt and Sudan.

Taharqa versus the Assyrians

Taharqa was the third sovereign of the Twenty-fifth Egyptian Dynasty; no monuments were left in the names of Alara, Kashta, or Piankhy within Egypt itself; but they were mentioned there, only occasionally, as genealogical references. Taharqa therefore succeeded Shabaqo and Shebitqo, as indicated on several royal monuments, notably stela V, erected in the temple of Kawa in regnal year 6 to commemorate the torrential rains and abundant floodwaters that the king's priest had successfully obtained from the god Amun. "Thus did I come from Nubia among the brothers of the king that His Majesty had summoned. While I was with him, he preferred me above all his brothers and all his children. I was raised above them by His Majesty. I won the heart of the *pât* [nobility] and I earned the love of each and every one. I was crowned in Memphis after the Falcon soared toward heaven." Stela IV, also from Kawa and dated the same year, offers a similar version of the event with the addition of a reference—also found elsewhere—to the wish expressed by Alara, the founder of the royal line, who had dedicated his sisters to the cult of Amun and had asked the god, in return, to crown their descendent. This reminder was linked to the construction work that the young prince had promised Amun of Kawa at the time of his coronation. "His Majesty sent his army to Gem-Aten, with a numerous team [of workers] and countless artists. A director of works accompanied them to oversee the work in this temple, while His Majesty was at Memphis."

This further reference to Memphis is significant. Not only is that where Taharqa was crowned, but he was still residing there when he ordered new work to be carried out on the temple of Amun in Kawa. It was clearly from Memphis that he sent workers and artists to build the new sanctuary. Taharqa left many proofs of the importance he placed on Memphis, the capital of the monarchs of the Old Kingdom. In particular, the stelae of the Serapeum erected during his reign indisputably confirm Taharqa's ascendancy over the Memphite clergy. This situation probably dated back to the reign of Shabaqo,

whose interest in Memphis is illustrated by his ordering that a stone copy be made of the main creation story as preserved by Memphite theologians: "This writing was copied out anew by His Majesty in the House of his father Ptah-South-of-His-Wall, because His Majesty found it to be a work of the ancestors which had been worm-eaten, so that it could not be understood from beginning to end. His Majesty copied it anew, so that it became better than it had been before, in order that his name might endure and his monument last in the house of his father Ptah-South-of-His-Wall for all eternity, as a work done by the son of Re [Shebitqo] for his father Ptah-Tatenen, that he might live forever." The various stelae dating from year 6 furthermore imply the success of a royal policy of gaining control of the Nile Delta, the main stronghold of opposition. They contain an allusion to an action of this kind in Lower Egypt, in which the future king allegedly participated while still a young man of twenty, alongside his predecessor, Shebitqo. Another stela refers to the deportation of people and princesses from Lower Egypt to Kawa in order to serve

Previous page:
Taharqa's forehead, adorned with the two uraei wearing the red crown and the white crown, respectively

Left:
Head of a statue of Taharqa from Thebes (Egyptian Museum, Cairo)

Right:
The sphinx of Taharqa from Kawa (British Museum, London)

A bust of Taharqa in red granite,
found at Tanis

Right:
Taharqa offering two *nu* vases to the
god Hemen (Musée du Louvre, Paris)

Amun there. The erection of one of these
year-6 stelae at Tanis and the discovery of a
bust of Taharqa in the grand temple of
Amun there suggests that the king resided
in this former capital of the Psusenne and
Sheshonq rulers, hence another city ideo-
logically representative of the Egyptian
monarch during the first half of the first
millennium BCE. The city also constituted
a logical base from which not only to
foment the rebellion of Phoenician cities
against their Assyrian overlords after the
death of Sennacherib, but also, starting in
677 BCE, to organize the defense of Egypt's
eastern frontier against Assyrian attacks.

Like the Kawa stelae, the Tanis stela
includes an account of the arrival of
Taharqa's mother in Egypt. "[My] mother
was in Nubia, the royal sister, sweet love,
royal mother, [Aba]la, [may she] live! I
was separated from her as a young man
twenty years old when I [left] with His
Majesty for Lower Egypt. And here she
has come, descending the river, to see
[me], after so many years." Although the
account then takes a mythological turn—
the queen mother playing the role of Isis
and Taharqa the role of Horus—it
includes more realistic passages suggesting
that this voyage was designed to honor the
great lady as much as possible. "Upper
and Lower Egypt, and all foreign nations
prostrated themselves before this royal
mother and made great festivities; the
grandest among them as well as the lesser,
they [acclaimed] this royal mother." The
explicit mention of Taharqa's age at the
time when he left Nubia to follow
Shebitqo to Egypt, where he would soon
be crowned Shebitqo's successor, was a
vary rare occurrence in Egyptian literature
(matched only by that of Amenhotep II on
the grand stela of the sphinx at Giza), and
it makes it possible to calculate the
approximate age of the king during the
main events of his reign.

145

Stela of Esarhaddon found at Zenjirli
(Near Eastern Museum, Berlin)

Right:
Relief from the palace of Assurbanipal,
Nineveh, showing the king on his
chariot (Musée du Louvre, Paris)

It was probably toward the fifteenth year of Taharqa's reign that he had engraved—on the back of the wall of the Annals of Thutmose III in the temple at Karnak—a major inscription in which the king laments the fact that the tribute from Khor was no longer sent to the temple of Amun. It shows that after having maintained a close relationship with the Lebano-Syrian coast, so necessary for receiving the wood and other materials needed for the kingdom's construction projects, Taharqa had lost control of this region traditionally allied with Egypt. It has been suggested that the great offering he made to Amun was a preliminary rite to an oracular consultation with the god (similar to the one made by Thutmose IV when he hesitated over an expedition to Nubia to suppress a rebellion in year 8 of his reign, and to those made by kings of the Third Intermediate Period, whose oracular texts were nearby in the temple of Amun). It is probable that after this ceremony Taharqa undertook some action in Palestine, which the god inevitably endorsed.

Taharqa was roughly thirty-six years old in 674 BCE, when he was defeated at Memphis by the Assyrian king Esarhaddon, as recounted by the latter's annals. "From the city of Ishkhupri, fifteen days' [march] from Memphis, his royal residence, I fought daily, without interruption [during] bloody encounters with Taharqa, king of Egypt and Kush, may all gods curse him. Five times I hit him with the point of [my] arrows, [inflicting] wounds [from which he should not] recover. Then did I lay siege to Memphis, his royal residence, and I conquered it in the space of half a day by using mines, tunnels, and assault ladders. I destroyed [it], I razed [its walls], I burned it down. His queen, his harem, Ushankhuru his heir, and the rest of his sons and daughters, his property and his goods, his horses, his cattle, his sheep, in countless numbers,

I carried off to Assyria." It is probably the young prince Ushankhuru who is shown kneeling, a rope around his neck, before Esarhaddon on the stelae at Nahr al-Kalb, Til Barsip, and Zenjirli, the latter bearing the inscription from which this passage is excerpted.

The Assyrian king also deported all the Egyptian and Nubian officials loyal to the pharaoh, and replaced them with his own men to govern the land under his control. Esarhaddon claimed to rule all of Egypt and Kush. Taharqa was seriously weakened, and had to withdraw to Thebes, from where he nevertheless continued to organize resistance in the Delta. A new clash was avoided in 669 due to the death of Esarhaddon in Palestine. Two years later, however, Esarhaddon's son and successor, Assurbanipal, learned that Taharqa had managed to recover control of Memphis and part of Lower Egypt. "Taharqa, king of Egypt and Kush whom Esarhaddon, king of Assyria, my own father, had defeated, and in whose land he had ruled—that Taharqa forgot the power of Assur, Ishtar, and the [other] great gods, my lords, and he trusted in his own strength. He marched against the kings and governors whom my father had appointed in Egypt. He entered and took up residence in Memphis."

Assurbanipal therefore decided to solve Assyria's Kushite problem once and for all. "Taharqa, king of Egypt and Kush, heard of the advance of my army, in Memphis, and called up his warriors for a decisive battle against me. Upon a trust[-inspiring] oracle [given] by Assur, Bel, and Nabu, the great gods, my lords, who always [march] at my side, I defeated the battle[-experienced] soldiers of his army in a great open battle. Taharqa heard of the defeat of his armies while in Memphis." The king's only recourse was to withdraw to Thebes while Assurbanipal captured Memphis and followed him to Upper Egypt. All the princes and governors named by Esarhaddon, who had fled during Taharqa's return, were reinstated in their respective posts by Assurbanipal. But they did not really want to find themselves subject to a foreign power after Taharqa's departure, and so they began to conspire and negotiate a compromise with the pharaoh. "Let there be peace between us and let us come to mutual understanding. We will divide the country between us; no foreigner shall be ruler among us."

Men loyal to Assurbanipal revealed this conspiracy to him, and most of the plotters were put to the sword, as were other leading figures of the towns concerned. An exception was Nekau, king of Sau (Sais) and of Memphis, whom Assurbanipal spared on condition that he swears an oath "on the life of the gods." After which the Assyrian king clothed Nekau in splendid garments, jewels, and royal insignia, then gave him a dagger inscribed with his name that represented a sign of his trust in his vassal and a reminder of the loyalty he was owed. He supplied Nekau with royal paraphernalia and an escort of trustworthy officers to help him in his task, namely to rule over the key city of Memphis as well as Nekau's former province of Sau; meanwhile, Nekau's son, Psamtik, was named governor of the central Delta province of Athribis.

In his description of his role in setting up the Twenty-sixth, or Saite, Dynasty, Assurbanipal referred to the fate of his former enemy, Taharqa, in rather vague terms. In fact, we know little of Taharqa's final years. Manetho's history traditionally dated the start of Nekau's reign in 672 BCE, when first set up by Esarhaddon; the reign only became effective with Assurbanipal's confirmation of it around 668. No official document with the name of the Saite monarch has yet been found. The two rival rulers died in the same year,

Taharqa's pyramid at Nuri

664 BCE, Taharqa shortly before Nekau. Unlike his predecessors, who built their pyramid tombs at al-Kurru, Taharqa erected his imposing pyramid at Nuri, the western necropolis of the ancient city of Napata, near the site of Sanam (see map on page 167).

Taharqa left behind many monuments in the major cities of both Sudan and Egypt. He indicated his devotion to Amun Lord of Pnubs by dedicating chapels to the god in the above-mentioned temple at Kawa, in the temple of Amun-the-Bull, Lord of Nubia at Sanam, and in the temple of Mut (B 300) at Gebel Barkal. The god is depicted as a ram-headed sphinx—called a criosphinx—lying on a bench beneath a jujube tree, sacred to Doukki Gel, which curves over his head as he breathes in a flowering bouquet. Therefore Amun's main temple at Pnubs—already mentioned on the abacus of a column in temple B 500 at Gebel Barkal—built for Amun of Napata

during Piankhy's reign, constituted a major sacred reference, as indisputably confirmed by the artistic quality of the statue of Taharqa found in the Doukki Gel cache, which is clearly superior to his colossus at Gebel Barkal.

Tanutamun and Psamtik I

Taharqa was succeeded by Tanutamun, as recorded once again in Assurbanipal's annals. "Thereupon Urdamane (Tanutamun), Shabaqo's son [variant: nephew], seated himself upon his royal throne. Thebes and Heliopolis he made his strongholds. He gathered together his forces. To battle with my troops stationed at Memphis he mustered his battle array." Whereas Assyrian sources seem somewhat uncertain about the identity of the new king's parents, Nubian sources refer to Queen Qalhata, wife of Shebitqo, sometimes as "his mother" and sometimes as "his sister"—that is to say, his wife. Near the victory stela that Piankhy erected in his temple to Amun at the foot of Gebel Barkal (B 500), Tanutamun set up a second monumental stela (now in the Egyptian Museum, Cairo). It recorded the details of his accession and the stages of his reconquest of Egypt. "Year 1 when the king was crowned [. . .] His Majesty saw in a dream two serpents, one on his right, the other on his left. His Majesty woke up, but could not find them. [His Majesty] said: 'What has happened to me?' He was told: 'You possess Upper Egypt—you must take Lower Egypt. The Two Ladies appeared on your head to give you the land in all its length and all its breadth. Let no one else share it with you!'"

It was the two tutelary goddesses of Egypt, who adorned the king's brow in the form of the two cobras, or double uraeus, ever since his coronation, who spurred Tanutamun to undertake the conquest of the Delta. He first went to the temple of Amun-of-the-Pure-Mountain, at Napata, where he made a large offering when the processional statue of the god appeared. Then Tanutamun embarked for

Elephantine and Karnak, where he renewed his vows before Khnum and Amun, respectively. He continued his voyage unhindered to Memphis, ordering the restoration of ruined temples along the way, re-establishing cult images, making divine offerings, and re-installing the clergy, as was traditionally done by Egyptian monarchs after each period of troubles. It was at Memphis that the first clash occurred. The text of the stela remains vague about the identity of his adversaries; we learn only that they perished in great number during a bloody carnage. Tanutamun captured Memphis, and issued instructions that a new entrance of gilded stone should be built for Amun at the Napata temple, to thank the god for his help.

Tanutamun then set off to confront the princes of Lower Egypt, but according his stela—known as the Dream Stela—"they went into their huts as rats go into their holes." He did not manage to engage in battle with any of them. He decided to return to Memphis and devise a new strategy. Just then he learned that his opponents were at the palace gates, ready to recognize his authority. Their spokesman was Pakrur, ruler of Saft al-Henneh in the eastern Delta, who pleaded the princes' cause. Tanutamun decided to spare them and released them to govern their respective cities. Nowhere on the stela is there any mention of Nekau, king of Sau and Memphis, who is generally assumed, following Herodotus, to have been killed during Tanutamun's capture of Memphis. Back in Nineveh, Assurbanipal learned of the situation and prepared a second expedition into Egypt for the following year. "Urdamane (Tanutamun) heard of my campaign and that I trod the soil of Egypt. He abandoned Memphis and fled to Thebes to save his life. The kings, princes, and mayors whom I had set up in Egypt came and kissed my feet. I took the road

Top, left:
Statue of Tanutamun from Gebel Barkal
(Sudan National Museum, Khartoum)

Top, right:
Relief carving of Tanutamun in
the chapel of Osiris-Ptah-Lord of Life,
Karnak

Far left:
Tanutamun's Dream Stela from Gebel
Barkal (Egyptian Museum, Cairo)

after Urdamane (Tanutamun) and marched to Thebes, his stronghold. He saw the approach of my terrible battle array and he fled to Kipkip." This latter town, unfortunately, has not been identified.

Thebes was sacked once again. But the Assyrian king halted there, content to return to Nineveh with substantial booty, including two obelisks of electrum. The reign of Psamtik I thus began with the death of his father, Nekau, but did not become effective over much of his territory until Assurbanipal had driven Tanutamun from Egypt. A historian of the second century CE, Polyaenus, claimed that Psamtik won a victory over Tanutamun near the temple of Isis in Memphis. It is therefore possible that Tanutamun tried to capture the capital one last time. And it is worth mentioning that up to year 8 of his reign, Theban inscriptions concerning the induc-

Sphinx of Psamtik I found in the Karnak
cache (Egyptian Museum, Cairo)

Right:
Statue of the Divine Adorer
Shepenwepet II found in the Karnak
cache (Egyptian Museum, Cairo)

tion of priests continued to date events from Tanutamun's reign; furthermore, the highest priestly functions in Thebes were still being filled by members of the Kushite royal family. It was only in year 9 that a major shift occurred, when Taharqa's daughter, Amenirdis II, the God's wife, adopted Nitokris, daughter of Psamtik, to be her successor in this crucial office. Unlike Taharqa, Tanutamun is never mentioned in Manetho's *Aegyptiaca,* which indicates that Egyptian historians preferred to consider Psamtik I as the sole true pharaoh during this transitional period.

Henceforth, Tanutamun ruled only over Nubia until his death at some unknown date. He was buried in the cemetery at al-Kurru, near Piankhy, Shabaqo, and Shebitqo, in a tomb with a painted interior, once topped by a small sandstone pyramid. Little is known about the personality of the last king of the Twenty-fifth Dynasty. The Dream Stela, the only major surviving inscription from his reign, is hardly revealing because it attempted to match the Victory Stela of his forebear, Piankhy.

One practice shared by all these monarchs, from Piankhy to Tanutamun, was the burial of their horses in a cemetery not far from their own necropolis at al-Kurru. Each animal was buried upright, in an individual grave adapted to its size. Twenty-four of these tombs have been found, aligned in four rows. This particular interest in horses is also mentioned in the Victory Stela set up by Piankhy, who was furious when he discovered the condition of the stables in Heliopolis. He said to the defeated king Nimlot, "As true as I live and as Re loves [me], as true as my nose is full of life, that my horses were made to hunger pains me more than any other crime you committed in your recklessness . . . ."

Despite the conflictory situation in which the Saite kings succeeded the Kushite

152

monarchs, Psamtik I positioned himself as the heir to the latter. Thus on the year-9 stela commemorating Nitokris's adoption as God's wife of Amun by Shepenwepet II, Taharqa's titulary was cited twice and suffered no later obliteration. Much later, in year 20 of Psamtik's long reign of over fifty-four years, a stela recording the death of the Apis bull explicitly mentioned that the sacred bull had been born in year 26 of Taharqa's reign. Psamtik seemed to have waited for favorable opportunities, avoiding confrontation, before replacing Kushite heirs in the south with more trustworthy men from the north. Montuemhat, the Fourth Prophet of Amun, had a surprising career: he was appointed *sarru* (prince) by the Assyrians when they reorganized the country during Esarhaddon's reign, yet remained a powerful man in Thebes throughout the reigns of both Taharqa and Psamtik I. Such prudence, notably concerning the clergy at Thebes and Memphis, among whom there were probably still many supporters of the Kushite kings, did not prevent the Saite king from adopting a number of measures to discourage any further designs on Egypt by the Napatan clan. He dispatched one of his best generals to Thebes, Djedptahiufankh, established a new garrison at Elephantine, and sent an expedition into Lower Nubia (at an unfortunately unknown date).

The import of this last piece of information, mentioned on a temple block at Edfu, is hard to assess, but it suggests a climate of wariness or tension at the very least, a mood possibly related to the recent defection of Egypto-Libyan troops. Herodotus reported that "two hundred and forty thousand Egyptians of fighting age" deserted and went into Ethiopia (as Sudan was called by classical authors and in the Bible). According to Herodotus, the defection involved soldiers garrisoned at Elephantine who were unhappy about

not being relieved for three years, and thus left the service of the pharaoh for that of the king of Napata. In fact, the true reason for the exile of these *asmakh* (deserters) seems to have been Psamtik's mistrust of the foreign troops. In fact his military policy was based on this suspicion. Herodotus added that the king of Ethiopia (Kush) "told them to dispossess certain Ethiopians with whom he was feuding, and occupy their land. These Ethiopians then learned Egyptian customs and have become milder-mannered by intermixture with the Egyptians" (II, 30). This incident might explain the reinforcement of Egyptian cultural models in Sudan at the time the new Napatan Dynasty was getting started.

Bust of Monthuemhat,
Fourth Prophet of Amun
(Egyptian Museum, Cairo)

The Early Years of the Napatan Dynasty

It was during the long reign of Psamtik I in Egypt that a new monarchy emerged in Sudan. Little is known of the early years of this so-called Napatan Dynasty. The dates of the reigns of each king, estimated by George Reisner on the basis of the size and wealth of their respective tombs, remain highly conjectural. Shortly after Psamtik I consolidated his power in the Theban region, around regnal year 12, Tanutamun died and was succeed by Atlanersa, son of Taharqa and a queen whose name has been only partly preserved as [. . .]salka. Although thereafter completely estranged from the throne of Egypt, the king adopted an Egyptian-style titulary with all five traditional names, only the birth name being of Kushite origin. This practice would continue to be respected in the court of Napata, followed by that of Meroe, down to the early centuries of the Common Era, even as Egyptian hieroglyphs would continue to be used as the official writing of the kingdom for several centuries longer.

Strangely, these kings would continue to be styled, in stereotypical fashion, as "Lord of the Two Lands" and "King of Upper and Lower Egypt" rather than as a function of the actual territory they ruled. They continued to wear the double uraeus. But whereas their predecessors liked to pride themselves on their double sovereignty over Egypt and Sudan, Napatan kings primarily claimed rights over the land they no longer held, only occasionally referring to their sovereignty over the Sudanese kingdom of Kush. Atlanersa apparently reigned for a decade or so, probably living in Napata where he built a temple to Amun (B 700) and left various other monuments such as an altar inscribed

Temple B 700, begun in the reign of Atlanersa, seen from the top of Gebel Barkal

with his complete titulary. The depiction of Amun of Pnubs on the temple pylon indicates that the sanctuary retained major significance at the time. Atlanersa was buried at Nuri, where a few remains of tomb furnishings have made it possible to identify the infrastructure belonging to his pyramid.

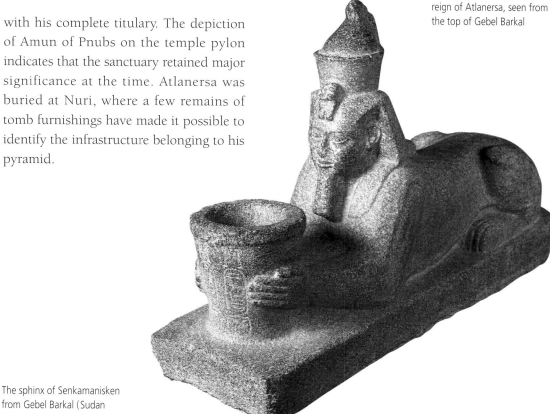

The sphinx of Senkamanisken from Gebel Barkal (Sudan National Museum, Khartoum)

Shabtis of Senkamanisken (Museum of Fine Arts, Boston)

Right:
Statue of Anlamani from Gebel Barkal (Sudan National Museum, Khartoum)

Far right:
View of Tell al-Maskuta in the eastern Delta, along the path of the canal begun by Nekau II

It must therefore have been around 643 BCE that Senkamanisken ascended to the throne; he reigned for approximately twenty years. We do not know how he was related to Atlanersa. He nevertheless completed the temple of Amun begun by his predecessor, engraved his name next to Atlanersa's on the altar, and was buried in a nearby grave at Nuri, all of which suggest strong family ties between the two kings. As a builder, Senkamanisken was highly active at Gebel Barkal and Sanam. We have little information about the historic context of his reign and the nature of his relationship with Egypt during that time. Only a fragment of a palette bearing the name of Senkamanisken, unearthed at Memphis in the early twentieth century, suggests that the countries maintained some kind of contact, the nature of which would be hard to determine. Meanwhile, the discovery of a deposit of votive objects bearing the king's name in the older strata of the temple of Amun in Meroe suggests that the city was already enjoying the favor of Napatan monarchs. We can therefore be certain that the kingdom extended from Pnubs, south of the third cataract, which remained an important religious center (as demonstrated by the two statues of Senkamanisken found in the cache of the temple of Amun) to Meroe, located between the fifth and sixth cataracts.

Anlamani's accession to power and a few significant events of his reign were inscribed on the so-called Coronation Stela that the king erected in the first court of the temple of Amun at Kawa. It was placed near, and inspired by, one of Taharqa's year-6 stelae, invoking a voyage by his mother, to whom he had sent some courtiers as escort; in it, she was compared to Isis meeting up with her son Horus. His mother, Nasalsa, was depicted behind the king on the stela; the date of the inscription has been lost. The text

refers in a rather vague manner to Anlamani's predestination for the throne since he was the eldest son of Atum, whom Amun had 'seen' in his mother's womb prior to his birth. Then the stela addresses more concrete subjects; a few references to some rebels that Amun "crushed for him in this land" and to the arrangements he made "in each province" during a trip to Gem-Aten suggest that troubles may have arisen during the transition between reigns. But the traditional phrasing employed here might merely be a revival of Egyptian models used earlier by Twenty-fifth Dynasty kings. At any rate, the inscription mentions a victorious campaign against the Blemmyes, in which Anlamani did not participate personally.

To celebrate the arrival of his mother, Nasalsa, at Kawa, Anlamani dedicated his four sisters to be sistrum players to the four great Nubian Amuns: Amun of Napata, of Gem-Aten, of Pnubs, and of Sanam. This concern for the temple of Amun at Pnubs is confirmed by the presence in the Doukki Gel cache of a truly exceptional statue of Anlamani. Along with the first statue of Senkamanisken, it is the only known statue of a Kushite or Napatan king wearing a *pschent* that retains the dimensions of Egypt's double crown. True enough, this powerful symbol of pharaonic monarchy would be found on the heads of the colossi at Tabo, but the style of those statues and the laurel leaves on the red crown had evolved a long way from Egyptian models. The presence of Amun horns along with the *pschent* is another sign of persistent ideological traditions borrowed from the northern neighbor, as also reflected in many of the phrases on the Coronation Stela.

It was probably during Anlamani's reign that Psamtik I died, in 610 BCE. He was succeeded by his son, Nekau II. This latter's reign, although it lasted a mere six years, was very revealing of the major transformations then occurring in the entire region. He left only a few commemorative monuments, mainly in Sau (Sais) where the Twenty-sixth Dynasty monarchs lived and were buried, so it was above all Herodotus and Diodorus who documented his reign. Nekau II undertook a vast construction project designed to allow boats to sail from the Mediterranean to the Red Sea by building a canal between the Pelusiac branch of the Nile and the Gulf of Suez. The canal, according to Herodotus, was "four days' voyage in length, and it was dug wide enough for two triremes to move in it rowed abreast. It is fed by the Nile, and is carried from a little above Bubastis by the Arabian town of Patumus; it issues into the Red Sea." He claimed that "a hundred and twenty thousand Egyptians died digging it. Nekau stopped work, stayed by a prophetic utterance that he was toiling beforehand for the barbarian" (II, 158).

Anlamani's pyramid
at Nuri

Indeed, the canal would be re-opened and completed at the order of the Persian king, Darius, less than a century later, as witnessed by several commemorative stelae erected along the canal. Certain passages of the inscriptions refer to the silting up of the canal along an eighty-four kilometer stretch when work was begun again.

Here Herodotus mentions the construction of triremes in the Mediterranean and the Red Sea, but it was in a passage of book four dealing with maps of the world that he revealed the exploratory voyage around Africa commissioned by the Nekau, thereby simultaneously acknowledging the success of the initial canal project. "When he had finished digging the canal which leads from the Nile to the Arabian Gulf, he sent Phoenicians in ships, instructing them to sail on their return voyage past the Pillars of Heracles until they came into the northern sea [i.e., the straits of Gibraltar and the Mediterranean Sea] and so to Egypt. So the Phoenicians

set out from the Red Sea and sailed the southern sea; when autumn came they would put in [. . .] at whatever part of Libya they had reached [i.e., the Atlantic coast of Africa] [. . .] so that after two years had passed, it was in the third that they rounded the pillars of Heracles and came to Egypt. There they said (what some may believe, though I do not) that in sailing around Libya they had the sun on their right hand (IV, 42)." This account gives an idea of the considerable expansion of the civilized world during that period, and naturally sparks further curiosity. The interest in maritime navigation and a desire to circumscribe the African continent was probably not alien to Egypt's eternal fascination with Black Africa.

Nekau II was famous above all for his military exploits on the eastern borders and in Asia, exploits known to us mainly from the Bible, Flavius Josephus, and the Chaldean chronicles. Despite the Egyptian army's crushing defeat at Carchemish,

Nekau managed to repulse Nebushadressar's troops, thereby saving Egypt from a Babylonian invasion that the prophet Jeremiah had foretold with great conviction. On the other side of the Euphrates, he laid the foundations of a new Asian empire that would have an important impact on his successors' foreign policies. At his death in 595 BCE, however, this empire was temporarily challenged by Babylon's victory over Jerusalem. Nekau was buried at Sau, along with the other Twenty-sixth Dynasty kings.

He was immediately succeeded by his son, Psamtik II. Although directly concerned by the events unfolding in the Near East, and although probably involved in the kingdom of Judah's resistance to Babylon, the new king was primarily concerned with the recurring issue of the relationship, now nearly a century and a half old, between the Egyptian and Kushite monarchies.

Sometime early in Psamtik II's reign, Anlamani died and was succeeded by his

Aspelta's Election Stela from Gebel
Barkal (Egyptian Museum, Cairo)

brother, Aspelta. The so-called Election
Stela erected in the first court of the temple
of Amun (B 500) at Gebel Barkal, near
Piankhy's Victory Stela and Tanutamun's
Dream Stela, recounts the specific circumstances of his accession. It reveals a
monarchic reality far different from the one
that prevailed in the days of Taharqa and
Tanutamun. No precise information survives on the way power passed from one
monarch to another after the Napatan
Dynasty withdrew into Sudan; we pointed
out that Anlamani's Coronation Stela refers
to his legitimacy only through highly
stereotyped metaphors. But with Aspelta
we learn that a new way of choosing the
king, through election, was envisaged. The
stela is dated from the first year of his reign,
the fifteenth day of the second month of
winter. The king and his entire army were
then in Lower Nubia, near a town located
immediately upstream from the second
cataract, but which has the same name—
"Pure Mountain"—as Gebel Barkal. The
incident clearly took place between
Aspelta's accession and coronation, "after
the falcon alighted on his *serekh*," the image
of the façade of the palace in which the
Horus name of the king was written.

The army was nevertheless unaware of
the identity of the new king. "No one
knows, except Re himself!" So a college
comprised of six army commanders, six
officials from the treasury, six overseers of
the archives, and seven overseers of the
royal seal—twenty-five men in all—was
formed to designate the new king.
Everyone agreed that this role really
belonged to the god Re, "because the king
is the image of Re among the living."
However, not knowing how to question
the sun god they turned to Amun-Re,
"Lord of the Thrones of the Two Lands
who resides in the Pure Mountain." The
members of the college therefore went the
temple of Amun-Re to consult him. After

Stela of year 3 of Aspelta's reign from Gebel Barkal (Musée du Louvre, Paris)

of the king's mother, who shakes two sistra in their direction. It should be noted that the names of Aspelta, Anlamani, and various members of the royal family that were mentioned in the scene as well as in the main inscription, were later chiseled out.

The weakening of monarchic power indicated by recourse to the election of a king by a college of senior officials was compensated by their acquiescence in favor of Re, the founder of royalty, and then to Amun of Napata, their dynastic god. The divine essence of the monarchy was thereby confirmed. But the political difficulties encountered by Napatan kings, already discreetly implied by Anlamani's Coronation Stela, were confirmed by a stela erected in Aspelta's regnal year 2, in the first court of temple B 500 at Gebel Barkal. This stone, known as the Excommunication Stela, contains a royal decree forbidding access to Amun's temple to a family of priests responsible for the death of an innocent person; furthermore, all of their descendents were excluded from ever holding a religious office. Although we do not know the context of this decree, the importance accorded to its commemoration implies that the incident behind the affair must have been fairly serious. Here again, the royal cartouches have been obliterated. In contrast, they are undamaged on several stelae dating from year 3, notably one bearing a decree of Queen Kheb's investiture as a sistrum player of Amun-Bull-of-Nubia at Sanam, a post previously held by Queen Madiken. Several pieces of another stela from regnal year 3 were found in the temple at Doukki Gel, but they are too fragmentary to permit us to determine the content of the main inscription.

prostrating themselves, they brought the king's brothers before the god, who failed to react. But when they presented Aspelta to him again, alone, Amun declared, "This one is the king, your lord, he is the one who will make you live, he will build all the temples of Upper and Lower Egypt, he will institute their divine offering [. . .]."

In order to receive the royal investiture, Aspelta then approached the god, who proclaimed, "The crown of your brother [Anlamani], king of Upper and Lower Egypt—justified! justified!—belongs to you. May it remain on your head, as shall remain on your head the Double crown and the *was* scepter in your fist, so that you [will be able to] overthrow all your ene-

mies." The borrowings from Egyptian terminology and ceremonial protocol are striking. The election was transformed into an oracular pronouncement by Amun of Napata whose unfailing commitment to the Kushite monarchy was explicitly stated: "He has been the god of Kush since the time of Re. It is he who guides us. The kingdom of Kush in his hands. He gives [it] to his beloved son!" Only in this passage is the actual identity of the realm revealed. The scene of investiture depicted on the stela, similar to those seen on the walls of Egyptian temples, occupies the upper zone of the stela. It shows Amun, with Mut behind him, placing the Kushite skullcap on the head of the new king in the presence

Right:
Top of the statue of Aspelta from Gebel Barkal (Museum of Fine Arts, Boston)

Aspelta erected a fifth stela in front of the south tower of the first pylon of the temple of Amun at Gebel Barkal. The pyramid that the king had built for Khaliut, one of the sons of Piankhy, and the donations he made to Khaliut's "house of millions of years" in terms of land, servants, and offerings of all kinds, reveal the importance that the Napatan monarchs placed on family ties with the Twenty-fifth Dynasty. Allowing the deceased prince to express his gratitude to his benefactor, the inscription draws endlessly from traditional Egyptian phraseology, notably supplying one of the latest attested uses of the expression "mansions of millions of years," employed in Egypt from the Thirteenth Dynasty to the Third Intermediate Period to refer to a royal religious foundation associated with monarchic rites or a divine sanctuary. The persistence of Egyptian ceremonial practices of a monarchic nature is illustrated once more by versions of the "treatise of the king acting as the sun priest" that figure on the covers of the sarcophagi of Anlamani and Aspelta at Nuri. This text, which appeared for the first time in Hatshepsut's temple in Deir al-Bahari, is attested during the reign of Amenhotep III in the temple of the royal *ka* at Luxor, and was later incorporated into the decorative scheme of Taharqa's building by the lake at Karnak, as well as in the large Theban tomb of a chief lector-priest, Petamenope, contemporary with this transitional period that covers the end of the Twenty-fifth and the beginning of the Twenty-sixth Dynasty. It is also worth noting that the inscriptions on Petamenope's *shabtis* parallel those on Taharqa's *shabtis*. Hence it seems indubitable that close cultural ties were maintained for some time after the separation of the Egyptian and Kushite monarchies.

Aspelta's sarcophagus
(Museum of Fine Arts, Boston)

Psamtik II's Military Expedition into Nubia

In Egypt, meanwhile, at a date difficult to pinpoint accurately but probably posterior to Psamtik I's regnal year 20 (when, as mentioned above, reference to the birth of an Apis bull explicitly mentioned year 26 of Taharqa's reign), a campaign was launched throughout the country to obliterate almost all Kushite royal names. At the same time, one of the two uraei on Kushite crowns, which recalled the domination of Nubian monarchs over Egypt, was systematically smashed on all reliefs and statues. Since the names were usurped by only one Saite pharaoh, the identity of the individual who issued this order is clear: Psamtik II. (In a few cases, the perpetrators even left intact the hieroglyphs that also figured in Psamtik's names, making usurpation all the easier.) This campaign, which concerned all Kushite monarchs whether or not they reigned over Egypt, was designed to eliminate

totally the Twenty-fifth Dynasty from Egyptian history—the dynasty was henceforth judged, ex post facto, to be illegitimate. The operation was all the more striking in that it occurred some seventy years after the Kushites had left; furthermore, as discussed above, there are very few extant signs in either Egypt or Sudan of tension or outright conflict between the two countries during that entire period.

The presence of the Kushite army in Lower Nubia, as indicated by Aspelta's Election Stela, is one of the strongest arguments in favor of military activity in the region, but the text of the stela is silent on that particular subject. And the exact location of the town where it took place, called Pure Mountain, can only be approximately determined as being somewhere in the sphere of influence of the god Dedun, between Kalabsha and Semna, perhaps somewhere around Abu

Simbel where a depiction of the temple of Amun of Napata within the Pure Mountain was carved on one wall of the great temple of Ramesses II. Probably some time after the accession of Aspelta, in year 3 of Psamtik II's reign, a messenger warned the Egyptian king that the Nubians were planning to attack, as stated on a fragmentary stela discovered at Tanis in a pit in the temple of Amun. "His Majesty sent an army to accompany the high officials of the Residence to the land of Shas," a region of Upper Nubia often cited in contemporaneous texts, notably in a long inscription in the temple of Taharqa at Sanam. Several other incomplete place-names are not currently identifiable, and the rest of the inscription contains many lacunae that make it impossible to quote at length.

The army reached the place of residence of the *kur*, the local term for king, near a city called Ta-Dehenet. This name, used in Egypt for natural high points that feature steep cliffs, appears in several Nubian texts. It might refer to Gebel Barkal itself or to other similar, if somewhat lower, buttes in the area. At any rate, that is where the bloodiest of the cited battles occurred. Several successive clashes took

Aerial view of the sacred mountain of Gebel Barkal, seen from the Nile

Right:
Head of a statuette of Psamtik II
(Musée Jacquemart-André, Paris)

Psamtik II stela found at Shellal, near the first cataract

Right: Facsimile of the inscription on the stela of Psamtik II

place, the victors being the Egyptian army which, according the custom and idiom of the day, "cut down the trees" of the vanquished peoples. A connection has already been suggested between the content of this stela and the destruction of the royal statues found in the Gebel Barkal caches described above. It was only the isolated nature of the statue-breaking phenomenon—at least until the Doukki Gel cache was found—that made scholars hesitate to favor this hypothesis over the competing theory of conflict within the Napatan monarchy itself.

The Egyptian military campaign is recorded in other sources. In addition to a brief passage in Herodotus (primarily interesting because it cites the incident as the most important event in Psamtik II's reign), Greek, Carian, and Phoenician graffito left on the legs of the colossi of Ramesses II at Abu Simbel by members of the expeditionary force help to mark the passage of the army and supply some additional information about its composition. Thus we learn that General Amasis was placed at the head of the of the Egyptian troops while General Potasimto commanded the Phoenician, Jewish, and Greek contingents—both figures are known from various monuments in Egypt. One inscription, for example,

explained that, "King Psamtik came to Elephantine, these words are written by those who sailed with Psammetichos [Psamtik], son of Theocles. They went upstream of Kerkis, as far as the river allowed. The foreigners were commanded by Potasimto, the Egyptians by Amasis." It has been suggested that the place-name Kerkis refers to Kurgus, meaning the old Egyptian border of Hagar al-Merwa during the New Kingdom. The unnavigable rapids mentioned in the text would therefore refer to the fourth or even fifth cataract. Since none of these inscriptions have been accurately dated, their exact place in the chronology of events is not easy to determine, especially since two other stelae present a different picture of this military campaign.

Indeed, a text very different from the one on the Tanis stela has survived in two copies, engraved on stelae of pink granite, found respectively near the second pylon at Karnak and to the north of the granite quarries of Shellal. The Karnak stela is in poor condition, but the surviving fragments suffice to prove that its text exactly corresponds to the one on the Shellal stela, which has survived intact. Unlike the Tanis version, a precise date is given: year 3, the second month of summer, the tenth day. Whereas in the first stela Psamtik II was busy restoring ruined temples and building new altars, here he was "strolling the marshes of Lake-of-Neferibre, traveling up and down its flooded stretches, crossing its two districts and gazing upon the sycamores of the Land of God" when suddenly a messenger arrived from Nubia. "His Majesty was told: 'The army that your Majesty sent to Nubia has reached the land of Pnubs. It is a land devoid of battle fields, a place devoid of horses.' Nubians from all parts had risen against him, their hearts full of anger [?] when he attacked those who had rebelled against him there; because he was furious at those who had risen against him. His Majesty took part in the combat as soon as he reached the battle. The rebels capitulated before a single arrow was unleashed against them. The hand wearied not and we waded in their blood as though [in] water. Those who tried to flee did not succeed and were brought back as prisoners: four thousand two hundred men."

The first question that arises concerns the exact whereabouts of Psamtik II when the messenger reached him. The Greek graffito at Abu Simbel, cited above, said he was staying at Elephantine. The marshy landscape mentioned on the stela is hardly in accordance with the surroundings of the first cataract, unless we are dealing with a mythological landscape here. In any case, the account is highly condensed; scarcely has the messenger begun to describe the situation when the king is suddenly in the midst of an extremely violent battle that took place in Pnubs, which we now know corresponds to Kerma and its hinterlands. The reference to a kind of broad coalition of the various Nubian peoples is very significant. It suggests an extensive Nubian reaction to early Egyptian victories around Napata, described on the Tanis stela, a reaction that triggered the sending of a messenger to Psamtik II and the king's personal involvement in the battle of Pnubs. It therefore seems incontrovertible that the military campaign occurred in stages. The successive phases of a conflict that unfolded in distinct regions were successively recorded in the stela of Tanis on the one hand and in those of Karnak and Shellal on the other.

It is unfortunate that the Tanis stela contains neither the month nor the day of the royal decision, which would have removed all ambiguity. Nevertheless, it is

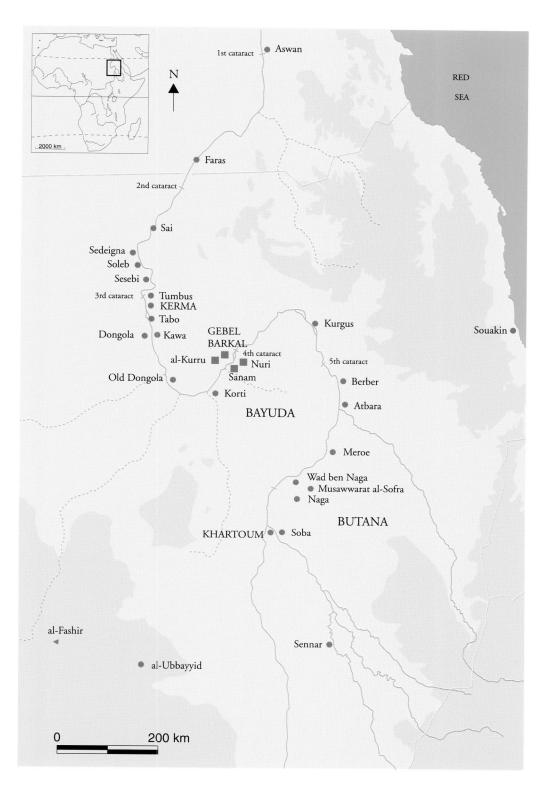

Map of Sudan

Bronze bowl inscribed with the name
of a priest of Amun Lord of Pnubs,
found in a Napatan tomb at Kerma

Right, top:
Graffito from Wadi Hammamat
showing a Divine Adorer

Right, bottom:
Offering bouquets to the victorious
Sety I, north wall of the hypostyle
hall, Karnak

clear that a new situation is being described, whereas the messenger mentioned in the other two stelae refers to an army that the king has already sent into Nubia. This army probably headed directly to the land of Shas, where it knew it would find the *kur*, perhaps taking the road already heavily traveled in the New Kingdom—as witnessed by graffiti left at various points along the route—from Korosko to Kurgus. The arrival at a bend in the Nile near Abu Hamed would correspond fairly well to the description found in the Greek inscription at Abu Simbel. Several bloody battles would then have taken place near the fourth cataract; the Egyptian army, followed the policy—presumably already implemented in Egypt itself—of execrating a Kushite monarchy that still claimed to be Egyptian. They arrogated its most sacred symbols, then set about smashing the royal colossi at the temples of Gebel Barkal, breaking not only the double uraeus but also the nose—in accordance with the Egyptian magic practice—thus depriving the depicted individual of the ability to breathe. Less certain, however, is the army's responsibility for obliterating certain names on several stelae, since the inscriptions on the royal statues suffered no damage.

The fighting would then have shifted to Pnubs, apparently in the presence of the king and perhaps with the support of fresh troops. This would have been the final act of a military campaign that took Egyptian troops to all of Nubia's royal residences, notably to Kawa where the temple of Amun of Gem-Aten was located. At the present time we have uncovered no indications of the Egyptian army's arrival

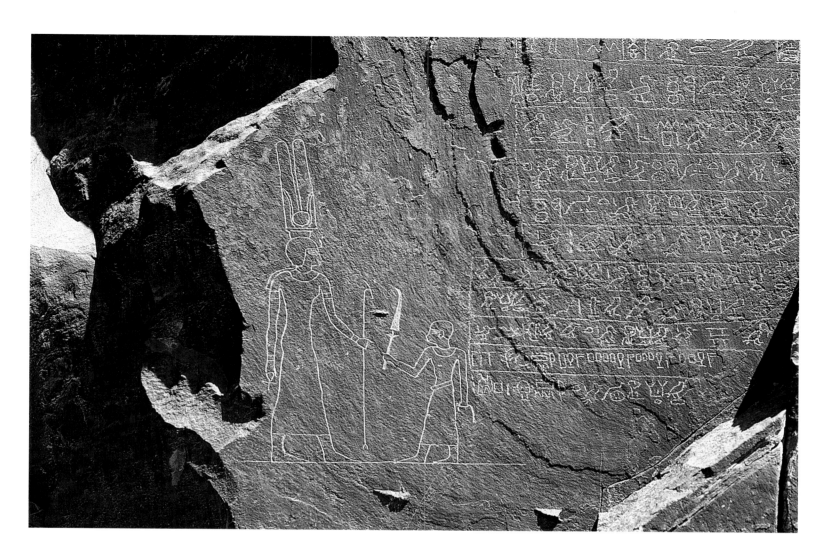

there, but it is not impossible that a cache similar to those at Gebel Barkal and Kerma will some day be uncovered.

The toppling of the statues at Doukki Gel must have occurred in conditions less favorable to the Egyptians than those at Napata, because the demolition was distinctly less radical. The uraei were barely touched (except on the second statue of Tanutamun), and noses hardly suffered (apart from the fall subsequent to decapitation). It was the *mekes* scepters that seemed to have been the focus of the soldiers' ire. Meanwhile, no chiseled obliterations from that period were found, when it came to inscriptions on statues or elsewhere on the site. We might wonder about the fate that befell Aspelta's year-3 stela, which was broken into pieces but in which the king's throne name—Merykare—was left intact. Given our current ignorance of the chronology of the Napatan Dynasty, we are unable to assert which year of Psamtik II's reign corresponds to the third year of Aspelta's reign.

The "great slaughter of large and small livestock" that the Saite pharaoh offered to the gods of Upper and Lower Egypt to thank them for insuring his victory is mentioned at the very end of the account and demonstrates once again that the stelae of Karnak and Shellal report the final phase of the campaign. Psamtik II would live for another three years. The exact date of his death is known from the Adoption Stela of the Divine Adorer Ankhnesneferibre: the twenty-third day of the first month of floods. It was during that time that he decided to go to "the land of Khor"'—the Syro-Palestinian plain—where Nekau II had retained a certain authority. During this voyage, Psamtik II received ceremonial bouquets from the principal deities, a practice attested in various places to celebrate a pharaoh's major victories, such as Sety I's campaign in

year 2, depicted on the north wall of the hypostyle hall of the temple of Amun at Karnak. Here it would seem to be a kind of triumphal tour by Psamtik II, following his military successes in Nubia, designed to enhance his prestige in regions favorable to him.

Although no date later than year 3 of Aspelta's reign has been found on any monument, specialists generally feel that Aspelta survived Psamtik II's campaign and reigned for another twenty years or so following his crushing defeat. This hypothesis rests primarily on an analysis of the king's tomb at Nuri. He nevertheless had two chapels built, one in the hypostyle hall of the temple of Taharqa at Kawa and the other in the temple at Sanam; he also built the first version of temple M 250, called the Sun Temple, at Meroe, where the remains of a broken stela have also been recovered. We do not know the exact date of the choice of Meroe—farther south than Napata and therefore beyond the reach of Egyptian troops—as the new capital of Nubia, but it is probable that Psamtik II's campaign produced a trauma that the Kushite authorities tried to assuage by getting farther away from their prickly neighbor. The period that immediately followed remains fairly obscure, but it is nevertheless likely that the caches at Gebel Barkal (Napata) and Doukki Gel (Pnubs) were made shortly after the destruction of the statues, both to provide them with a decent burial and to remove the shameful traces of the punishment inflicted by Egypt on kings who dared to retain pharaonic regalia to which they no longer had a right. In any case, the perfect condition of the statues at Doukki Gel, plus the presence of an enormous quantity of gold leaf in and around the pit, indicates swift action on the part of priests of the temple of Amun following the departure of Egyptian troops.

The erasures on some of Aspelta's monuments are harder to interpret. They basically occur on two stelae, dated year 1 and year 2, respectively. As mentioned above, both were found in the first court of the temple of Amun (B 500) at Gebel Barkal. On the first stela the face of the king's mother and all the cartouches in the scene at the top and in the text have been obliterated. On the second, only the figure of the king was defaced and subsequently re-carved, whereas all the cartouches were obliterated. Although there can be no doubt about the identity of the king and his mother on the first stela, in so far as the three other names of the royal titulary were left intact, the same is not true of the second stela. We might also wonder why the figure of the king was restored whereas the cartouches remain empty; the latter might have been redone in plaster, which later disappeared. The breaking into small pieces of two other Aspelta stelae, at Doukki Gel and Meroe, might have occurred at any time, totally unconnected to the reign itself. On the other hand, the fact the Aspelta's name remains intact on two stelae dated year 3 and on the stela to Khaliut suggests either that the reasons behind the first erasures were no longer valid in year 3, or that smashing was considered an alternative to the obliteration of names. The removal of names concerned not just the king but also the women of the royal family who transmitted authority and it occurred both on a monument attempting to establish the legitimacy of a clearly contested reign and on a record of an internal quarrel that degenerated into murder. Such obliterations therefore point to an affair within the Napatan court, directly concerning the subjects addressed in the two stelae.

However long Aspelta actually reigned, it is clear that he managed to overcome the political difficulties he encountered in

the first two years. Psamtik II's victorious campaign, leading to the destruction of royal statues at Napata and Pnubs, probably occurred early in his reign and did not prevent him from ruling once the Egyptians left, as indicated by the lavishness and quality of his tomb and its furnishings. The only surviving statue that postdates these events is the sphinx at Defeia, near Khartoum, which would seem to confirm the pursuit of building projects in the southern part of the country, where Aspelta restored a temple of Osiris. He would nevertheless be buried in a pyramid at Nuri, as would some fifteen Napatan kings after him, and the name of one of his foundations could still be found, two and a half centuries later, on the stela of the last of the line, Nastasen. Aspelta's immediate successor, Aramatelqo, was probably his son by Queen Kheb. A statue of Aramatelqo in festive *sed* dress, found at Merawi, shows that the punishment meted out by the Egyptian army did not totally inhibit Kushite kings from employing a cultural repertoire that they still considered their own. The inscription on the back pillar declared Aramatelqo to be "beloved of Amun-Re-Harakhty," while the inscription on the base includes an image of lapwings, which commonly symbolized the Egyptian peoples subject to the pharaoh. For many generations to come, the rulers of Napata, then of Meroe, would continue to call themselves kings of Upper and Lower Egypt.

Statue of Aramatelqo in jubilee dress
(Aegyptisches Museum, Berlin)

RITUAL DEPOSITS IN EGYPT
AND NUBIA

There were countless statues of wood, bronze, and stone in the temples and tombs of the Nile Valley. Given the vagaries of a turbulent history wracked by civil wars and invading armies, these works encountered diverse fates, and rarely survived intact into the present. Many can be seen today in the world's great museums, but local workshops certainly produced far more of them. Depictions of kings and deities—of varying dimensions depending on their function—were juxtaposed with portraits of high officials, priests, scribes, and even modest individuals. During excavations such as those conducted at Kerma, archaeologists are often amazed at the profusion of statues. Usually, however, they are small-scale statuettes, that had been systematically broken by looters and gold hunters. Some groups of statues nevertheless enjoyed a better fate, having had benefited from special treatment designed to allow them to remain in holy ground once they were deconsecrated. Also, inscribed or decorated blocks of stone belonging to earlier edifices were often incorporated into the walls of succeeding temples; sometimes entire sections of wall would be preserved for their religious value, and then integrated into a new building, which was thereby tied directly to a very ancient architectural tradition. Nor is it unusual to find one or several statues, generally fragmentary, built into a wall, thereby providing the edifice with some indirect protection. In certain religious buildings, the entire foundation or body of the structure might be composed of reused stones. Statues themselves might be cut into blocks to be used for construction. Such decisions were not based purely on a need for building materials, but also on a concern for monarchic continuity and on the respect that always accrued, despite everything, to sacred objects. Statues steadily filled the various rooms and courts of the temples—some of them might remain on their original spot for decades, centuries, indeed several millennia. Removing them was usually the result of special circumstances.

Caches

The increasing number of statues and the clutter they caused probably spurred priests and builders to reorganize the space at regular intervals. In certain cases, sculptures might be discarded, along with stelae and liturgical furnishings; such items were forgotten and eventually vanished. During disturbances sparked by more or less heavily contested regional and international conflicts between kings, princes, or military chieftains, and also during cataclysmic events such as earthquakes and devastating fires, the objects of worship in temples might be seriously damaged. They therefore had to be replaced or refurbished. Even when partly damaged, a statue retained its sacred quality. It therefore received care, and new layers of paint might be applied to restore its dignity. The various restorations and usurpations visible on many statues demonstrate that they were able to live many lives.

A 'cache' is a sacred store for precious objects that deserved respect and protection. The work of digging deep pits on temple grounds, in order to preserve diverse fragments or entire statues, was

Previous page:
View of the grand temple
of Amun (B 500) built by
Piankhy at Gebel Barkal

The Doukki Gel cache

175

Left:
The Karnak cache during excavations by Georges Legrain

Right:
A reconstructed statue of Amenhotep III from North Karnak

certainly not undertaken solely to get rid of clutter. Some of these pits, of course, might have originally been dug to provide earth for mud bricks used in reconstructing the temples. However, the location of the caches is not random, since they are usually found inside or very near the temple. Whether in a courtyard, under a dromos, or in outbuildings, these deposits fulfilled several functions that are not easy to determine. When a find can be dated, it is possible to offer an interpretation that fits the historical facts. Up till now, however, no text or depiction of this practice has provided hard information on the existence of a relevant ritual.

The most famous cache was discovered at Karnak on December 26, 1903, by French archaeologist Georges Legrain. While clearing the surface of a court to the north of the seventh pylon, the excavator uncovered pits from various eras and descending as deep as fourteen meters.

This find turned up hundreds of inscribed objects and statues, nine thousand statuettes and various fragments of bronze, as well as items in wood that were sometimes gilded. Contending with incredible difficulties, due above all to variations in the water table, the contents of the cache were inventoried, photographed, and then shipped to the museum in Cairo, where Legrain was finally able to catalogue and analyze them in the *Catalogue Général*. It took nearly four years to clear the bulk of the archaeological find, some of which is still in situ. Many questions remain, and the pit itself may yet deliver a great deal of information, in addition to the material already brought to light.

But this vast dump beneath the 'cache courtyard' will likely remain a puzzle. Study of the successive phases suggests that Egyptians probably began burying the material in the seventh century BCE. It has been suggested that the earliest caches

might have been deposited following the Assyrian sack of Thebes. Yet various clues indicate that Psamtik II lost interest in the former southern capital, which was still in the hands of partisans of the Kushite monarchs. The presence of several statues of Kushite kings with obliterations probably dating, as argued above, to the reign of Psamtik II, implies that the cache must have been buried after those events. The placing of the last statues in the cache must have occurred shortly before the start of the Common Era. It is remarkable that over a period of several centuries major work could have been undertaken here to store various categories of royal, divine, and private statues. The court lies in the heart of the architectural complex of Karnak, right near the junction of two axes: the main east–west axis running from the Nile to the sanctuary of the god Amun and the north–south axis linking the ceremonial palaces to the royal *ka*

temple in Luxor. It is on the latter axis that the cache lies.

On the same site of Karnak, but somewhat to the north, in front of the monumental gate leading to the enclosure of the temple of Montu, deposits of two royals statues of Amenhotep III were found underneath the dromos. This small cache, although partly re-opened at a later date, seems to predate or be contemporaneous with the construction of a small chapel that holds two Ramesside statues at the back. The statues of Amenhotep III were smashed into countless fragments following a fire. Shortly after this incident, all the fragments were placed in two perfectly organized square pits, 1.15 meters per side. The heads of the statues were set in the middle of the cache, while the feet were placed in the corners. Recovery of thousands of fragments has proven that each square contained the fragments of only one statue. Among the rubble in the west section were found Roman coins from the late first and second centuries CE. Also at Karnak, but in the middle of the platform on the western quay, three statues from the Middle and New Kingdoms were thought by excavators to be a foundation deposit. Analysis of inscriptions on the quay links the deposit of the cache to the period ranging from the Twenty-second to the Twenty-fifth Dynasties.

In January 1989 an oval pit 3.8 by 3 meters, some 2.5 meters deep, was unearthed by Mohammed El-Saghir, Director of Pharaonic Antiquities, in the peristyle court of the temple of Amenhotep III in Luxor. Twenty-six statues of gods and kings, in very good condition, were pulled from the mud and soil. Of very high artistic quality, most of these pieces date from the New Kingdom but two of them belong to the Twenty-fifth Dynasty, which might suggest that the pit was dug during the Late Period. Study of the pottery furnishings

Left:
Statue of Amenhotep III
as Amun from the
Luxor cache

finally led El-Saghir to hypothesize that the cache was made during the Roman era, between the first and second century CE. Once again, it appeared that the cache had been deposited, or at least was still in use, at a very late date. As at Karnak, the cache posed complex chronological problems, perhaps due to successive interventions or to a ritual that might have involved a later re-opening (which, however, remains to be demonstrated).

When it comes to Sudan, several publications have reproduced photographs of the "Roman baths" at Meroe, where archaeologist John Garstang and his wife exhumed statues from the bottom of a large pool. This was thought to be a cache organized after the destruction of the Meroitic edifice, but later closed again. These old excavations from the early twentieth century have recently been published, and it now looks as though the remains might have belonged to a temple dedicated to a water cult. The burying of nearly sixty fragmentary statues seems to have been done relatively quickly, but it should be noted that the deposit was more or less organized and that care was taken to protect items sculpted in poor-quality sandstone. A building, perhaps religious, would later have been erected on this sacred spot. Also from Meroe comes an extraordinary head of Emperor Augustus, found in front of a small temple (M 292), buried in a pocket of sand 2.5 meters below the surface. This prize piece of Roman sculpture was probably looted during an expedition by Meroitic armies down to Aswan, and then cached at Meroe at a later date—temple M 292 was rebuilt at least five times. In the entrance court to the temple of Taharqa at Tabo, mentioned above, another discovery might also have been the product of a cache buried hurriedly during a threat of major political upheaval. A single royal statue, in bronze

Right:
A Meroitic statue at
Tabo at the time of
discovery

The cache at temple B 500 at Gebel Barkal during excavation by George Reisner

but covered in carved plaster and gold leaf, lay in a simple ditch covered with sand. This royal portrait has been dated circa 200 BCE.

These few examples hardly represent an exhaustive list, yet they suffice to show that each cache constitutes a special case and that we cannot draw universal conclusions about the precise role of these ritual deposits. The variety of these finds must be stressed, as well as the difficulty of comparative analysis—the key point

involves the problem of dating each intervention, including the determination of whether or not the ensemble was reorganized at any subsequent point in time: the reopening of votive pits, well attested in the Greco-Roman world, may have already been practiced in the Nile Valley. Several pits dug in a sector designed to that end may have been used and then abandoned, as suggested by the holes on both sides of the cache at Doukki Gel. The same is probably true of the peristyle court in the

temple of Luxor. Evidence of deliberate destruction of statues is attested only in very rare cases. Several deposits have yielded sculptures in remarkably good condition, while on other occasions it is clear that the pieces suffered damage resulting from a violent incident.

As to the caches discovered by George Reisner at Gebel Barkal, they assume new significance in the light of the excavations at Doukki Gel. It is worth recalling, first of all, that statues of an identical set of kings were found in caches at two different sites some two hundred kilometers apart. The caches were located near the first or second court of a temple. The statues suffered the same kind of damage that targeted the power of a specific group of monarchs. The statues were all broken in an almost identical way, and such breakage cannot be attributed to the collapse of the building housing them, as has been suggested. The preparation of the pit to the southeast of temple B 500, which is similar in size to the others—four meters by two meters—has been chronologically pinpointed by stratigraphic analysis, but we lack extensive knowledge of the building that stood on that spot. Photographs of the Gebel Barkal caches reveal an intention to arrange the pieces in a certain order, as was the case at Doukki Gel, the heads being placed at the bottom and the bodies forming an intermediate layer. It seems clear that certain pieces were moved and have vanished, although the pits were not entirely emptied.

Pinnacle of rock in front of the cliff
of Gebel Barkal

The second cache at Gebel Barkal is located in annex B 904 of temple B 800. The sculpted fragments were set directly on the flagstones of this two-columned room, but here again they obey a certain order that seems to betray a desire to safeguard and shelter the pieces. Thus all the bases lie to one side, whereas the bodies are grouped a little way off. Several heads are missing, but the cache was not intact—holes and ditches made by treasure hunters came to light during excavation. The entire cache and the adjoining rooms were then covered to a depth of seventy centimeters with black soil that hid a number of other objects including amulets, faience vases, beads, and small fragments of statues probably coming from the spot where the royal portraits originally stood. Pieces of burned beams made of palm trees were also included in the fill, suggesting that this sector had burned. These statues were therefore accompanied, as at Doukki Gel, by remains associated with their original location.

Temple B 800 was rebuilt in stone shortly after the cache was sealed. Its plan is unusual because the architect took the cache into account, sealing it with a new annex that extended outward at the expense of the second court with lateral colonnades. The enlarged hall was occupied anew, and rites could be performed there. As at Doukki Gel, we see that the function of the annex was retained and that for two or three centuries priests remained aware of the importance of the caches. It is even possible that other ritual deposits were made here as a function of the needs of the cult.

Egyptian and Nubian Statues from Kerma.

The vestiges of statuary found on the various sites at Kerma constitute an apparently disconcerting group. No Nubian figurine or statue produced between the Neolithic age and the Classic Kerma Period has yet been uncovered. The few fragments of Egyptian stone vases and statues dating from the Sixth Dynasty and the early Middle Kingdom might have been brought to Kerma during official embassies or missions. Most of the Egyptian sculptures unearthed in the Nubian city and its necropolis, however, are contemporaneous with the late Middle Kingdom and Second Intermediate Period. Some of these items were found by Richard Lepsius in the nineteenth century in the religious complex that formed the heart of the city, but most of the statues exhumed during Reisner's excavations had been placed in funerary chapels and above all in the large tumuli of the last kings. All these statues and statuettes seem to have been made for sanctuaries or tombs in Upper and Middle Egypt, to judge by the inscriptions carved on them, which allude to various towns between Elephantine and Cusae. It is probable that at least some of them were brought back by Kushite armies during forays into Egypt, for which some Egyptian evidence survives.

However they made their way to Kerma, these objects seem to have constituted a kind of permanent heritage used in varying ways that are not always easy for us to reconstruct. Their status has often been compared to that of Egyptian statues re-employed during the same period by the Hyksos at Avaris or scattered across much of the Near East. Yet it is important to point out a major difference between the

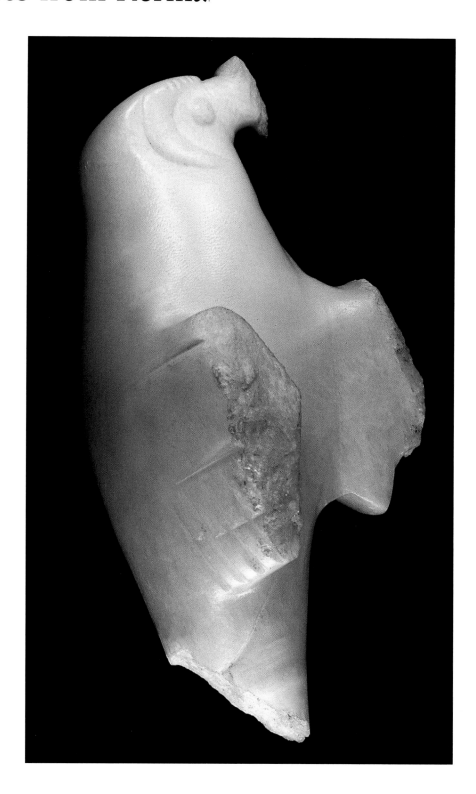

Calcite falcon from an Old Kingdom royal statue, found in the necropolis at Kerma (Museum of Fine Arts, Boston)

183

Head of a Middle Kingdom royal statue,
found in the necropolis at Kerma
(Museum of Fine Arts, Boston)

Statue of Lady Sennuwy, wife of the
nomarch Hepdjefa, found in tumulus III at
Kerma (Museum of Fine Arts, Boston)

two sets of objects: whereas Hyksos
monarchs usurped the portraits of Egyptian kings, there is no indication of a similar practice in Kerma, where the most
striking use made of these statues was,
without a doubt, the inclusion of a significant proportion of them in three huge
grave tumuli. Despite the fact that even
before Reisner began his excavations a
massive intrusion of looters had moved
many things around, it is possible to identify the original location of objects in
tumulus K III, which held some forty
more or less complete statues, and also in
K X, which held another thirty, plus a
dozen more lying nearby. In both cases, the
statues were found very near the burial
chamber and in the central corridor,
whereas in tumulus K IV the fifteen fragments of private statues discarded by robbers were scattered on the surface. It
should be pointed out that despite the condition of most of these statues today, they
were probably whole when they were

placed in the tombs. Recent research has made it possible to assemble fragments that were separated and dispersed by antiquities smugglers, subsequently ending up in different museums. This was the case with a kneeling statue of Sobekhotep VI, a Thirteenth Dynasty monarch, the largest part of which was purchased in 1889 by the Aegyptisches Museum in Berlin, while two connected pieces that formed the front of the base, uncovered during Reisner's digs, wound up in the storerooms of the Museum of Fine Arts in Boston. The causes of such damage are multifarious. A seated statue of Lady Sennuwy, wife of a monarch named Hepdjefa (now in the galleries of Boston's Museum of Fine Arts) remained intact in the central corridor of tumulus K III until it was unearthed. Yet the statue was riddled with multiple fissures, probably due to the alternating extremes of day and night temperatures and humidity in the desert climate to which it had been subjected for several millennia. The hunt for gold, which medieval lore held was hidden in the core of ancient monuments, was also responsible for the destruction of many of them.

The presence of private and royal Egyptian statues in Kerma's vast tombs relate to original burial practices that apparently came into use toward the end of the Classic Kerma Period. The large grave excavated under the modern town, which might be considered the last burial of a powerful king of Kerma, also contained several fragments of them, though it yielded only meager material, having been thoroughly looted. It is obviously risky to try to interpret rites that were practiced over a relatively short period in the context of a culture that we know little about, particularly so considering the absence of texts that might reveal their content and meaning (as is the case in Egypt). However, the discovery of several hundred sac-

Terracotta bust of a man from a pit in the Nubian town of Kerma

rificial victims in those same central corridors of tumuli K III and K X suggests that the statues, like the victims, glorified the deceased king and accompanied him into the afterlife. Egyptian statues in Nubia would serve as local models during the Twenty-fifth Dynasty and the Napatan Dynasty that succeeded it.

Also dating from the Classic Kerma Period is a terracotta bust of a man found in a pit near the last palace in the city, which just might represent one of the local princes. At any rate, it is the sole example to come to light in this region of

Fragmentary ram-headed sphinx
of glazed quartz (Museum of Fine
Arts, Boston)

Mut (B 300) at Gebel Barkal and the temple of Amun at Sanam, then on Atlanersa's pylon in temple B 700. A human-headed sphinx, also of glazed quartz, was discovered by Georges Legrain in the cache at Karnak, and both its style and technique evoke the Kerma sculptures, although how it came to be at Karnak remains to be explained.

In addition to statues that found their way to Lower Nubia once it was annexed by Egypt during the Middle Kingdom, and to Middle and Upper Nubia during the Second Intermediate Period (among which no divine portraits have yet been uncovered), there were the many royal and private statues made in Egypt or in Nubia itself during the New Kingdom. The architectural projects undertaken throughout Nubia during Taharqa's reign sometimes coincide with the creation of deposits of statues—at Semna, for instance, a cache contained small royal and private sculptures dating from the Middle Kingdom. In Taharqa's temple at Tabo, a seated figure of Sobekhotep IV was still in situ in the early twentieth century, in front of the southern pier of the second pylon. Elsewhere, at Gebel Barkal, Reisner unearthed another statue of the monarch Hepdjefa and several monumental statues that Piankhy had taken from the temple of Amenhotep III at Soleb in order to place them in the temple of Amun (B 500): a standing portrait of the king, a ram, the goddess Selket as a serpent and the falcon god Soped wearing on his head four frontal plumes, prefiguring the Onuris headdress worn by the colossi of Taharqa, Anlamani, and Aspelta.

At the time of writing, excavation of the temples at Doukki Gel has also yielded some fifty fragments of Egyptian statues, of which at least forty predate the New Kingdom. Although most of the surviving inscriptions fail to provide precise dating

an indigenous, free-standing human figure made prior to the first millennium BCE. In the cemetery, meanwhile, another group of statues, probably divine in nature, was found in tumulus K III and the neighboring temple K II. The statues in question were fairly large and represented animals in glazed quartz, of which various fragments have survived: two scorpions, the body of a crocodile, the body of two lions, and a ram's head. It is possible, for that matter, that the ram's head should be connected to one of the lion bodies, thus constituting the oldest known depiction of a 'criosphinx,' a form of Amun known as Amun of Pnubs. Amun would be depicted thus from the Twenty-fifth Dynasty onward, notably during Taharqa's reign in the temple of

Head of an Eighteenth Dynasty king, perhaps Thutmose IV, found in the Doukki Gel cache

Right:
Lower part of a statue of an overseer of cavalry found in the Doukki Gel cache

information, it is clear that we are dealing with documentation of the same type discovered by Reisner at Kerma. Because most of these fragments have been recovered from disturbed strata, it is hard to reconstitute their itineraries within the site or to understand how the Kushites might have used them prior to the founding of the Egyptian town during the first half of the Eighteenth Dynasty. Many, however, were found beneath the east temple of the Napatan Period, notably the statue of a treasury official named Renseneb, probably from the Thirteenth Dynasty. Also worth mentioning is an incomplete statuette of a certain Iymeru (son of another Iymeru who was vizier to that same dynasty), which was found in a layer of post-Meroitic demolition, suggesting that these remnants of ancient Egyptian monuments were involved in several phases of these buildings' lives, down to a relatively late date. Most of the fragments that have come to light—from the various sectors excavated from digging season to digging season—belonged to very fine statues made either of granite, *bekhen*-stone from Wadi Hammamat, or calcite. Obviously in much better condition during the Twenty-fifth Dynasty and Napatan Period than they are today, they constituted a veritable conservatory for sculptors working for Kushite kings, just as the old temples and necropolises of Egypt contained inspiring models for artists working under the Saite pharaohs.

Of special interest are two of the fragments from the Doukki Gel cache that are not part of the seven large royal Kushite statues. One is the head of a royal statue from the New Kingdom; the other is the lower section of a seated individual. The head is very fine in quality and shows the face of a sovereign from the first half of the Eighteenth Dynasty, probably Thutmose IV. The seated figure, an overseer of cavalry from the same period, bears several somewhat clumsy inscriptions. On the sides of the cubic chair they have become almost illegible, but the beginning of the inscription running vertically down the front of the cloak is clear: "everything that comes from the altars of [Amun] of Pnubs." the obliteration of the name of Amun indicates that the statue predates the Amarna Period when Akhenaten's agents erased the god's name from every available monument in Egypt and Nubia. As to Pnubs, it represents one of the oldest known references to this place-name, which would be largely attested from the Twenty-fifth Dynasty and into the Napatan and Meroitic Periods. A second attestation, fairly contemporaneous with the first, can be found on a small stela unearthed with a group of personal devotional objects to the west of the great temple of Amun, mentioned above.

The presence of these older items in the Doukki Gel cache is intriguing, especially since the same was true at Gebel Barkal where a statue of Thutmose III was set on the altar of Atlanersa, near one of the caches that also contained the lower part of a statue of one of Akhenaten's viceroys. Without wanting to speculate on the presence of such objects in deposits made on two major Nubian sites during the reign of Aspelta, it would seem that these items dating from the founding or early history of these towns were considered sufficiently precious to be added to the main contents of all three caches. The same was probably true of the other two fragments, a falcon head and a woman's bust, but their condition does not allow us to grasp their precise significance in the eyes of priests of the day.

The Birth and Consecration of Statues in the Mansion of Gold

Since earliest antiquity Egyptians equated the sculpting of a statue, whether divine or royal, with giving birth. Their phrase for "fashioning a sculpture" was literally "to give birth." Once completed, a portrait had to be brought to life by a rite called "the opening of the mouth"; this rite was also performed on mummies by a priest using a hooked adze, which breathed new life into the deceased. Creation and life-giving took place in a temple's "Mansion of Gold," a kind of alchemical laboratory where a statue was transformed into a medium that could receive the earthly worship due to a god or king. The oldest surviving references to the opening of the mouth date to the reign of Khufu. The ancient forms of the ritual can be intuited through later versions that have been preserved. Initially, it was the artisans themselves who proceeded to open the mouth of the statue they had just created. Later, this role was the prerogative of certain categories of priest, notably the *sem* priest who wore a characteristic panther skin when performing his rites.

Left:
Painting from the Theban tomb
of Huy, sculptor of Amun, usurped by
the priest Kenro, showing the ritual of
the opening of the mouth being
performed on his mummy

Top:
Depiction of the treasury in the Theban
tomb of the scribe of Amun, Kenro

Detail of the House of Gold from
Kenro's tomb

Top:
View of Thutmose III's House
of Gold at Karnak

Bottom:
View of Shabaqo's House
of Gold at Karnak

The paintings on the walls of certain New Kingdom tombs in Thebes illustrate the making of statues and the rituals performed on them. The Ramesside tomb of the scribe Neferrenpet, called Kenro, included a schematic depiction of the Mansion of Gold and Treasury of Amun, of which Kenro was overseer. A monumental gate framed by the two piers of a pylon lead to an interior divided into two zones. The first is composed of a courtyard where porters are addressed by the gate-keeper, who holds a whip; at the back of the court are two buildings, the larger of which has a painter decorating a statue, a burial mask, and several statuettes. A second monumental gate, aligned with the first, leads to a second zone where Kenro, the scribe of Amun's Mansion of Gold, is pictured three times larger than the other figures; there he "receives the work of artisans of the domain of Amun-Re, king of gods." Six registers of the wall painting feature the artisans at work; the leading artist is called the "chief sculptor."

The actual ritual of opening the mouths of statues can be followed step-by-step in the funerary chapel of Rekhmira, vizier to Thutmose III. Each stage of the ritual, performed here for a private individual, is depicted in a separate scene. The text of the ritual records a dialogue between the participants, as in the Pyramids Texts. It is titled, "Performing the opening of the mouth for the statue of N. in the Mansion of Gold." As adapted for statues and private mummies, however, the surviving versions steadily supplemented the original liturgical rites with funerary practices absent from earlier forms, initially designed exclusively for portraits of kings and gods. The spot where these rites were performed has been identified in the temple of Amun at Karnak. During Thutmose III's reign, they were conducted in a long hall with concealed entrances, set between two walls to the north of the contemporaneous part of the temple. Later, given building extensions to the west, the Mansion of Gold was shifted to the northeast of the hypostyle hall. It was restored during the Twenty-fifth Dynasty by Shabaqo, who had the columns engraved with a dedication that revealed the name and function of the building: "A Mansion of Gold, like something new, to give birth to [statues of] gods of the South and North, and to open their mouths, after His Majesty found that it was falling to ruin." When first discovered, this hall appeared to be a paved hypostyle hall of which only the vestiges of four rows of columns remained.

The Ptolemaic temple of Hathor at Dendera contains the sole complete example of a liturgical Mansion of Gold. The room, small in size, is located on the sixth landing of the west staircase that climbs from the outer vestibule. The entrance to the room is engraved with a text setting out the rules of operation: "As to the Mansion of Gold and the giving birth of *akhemu*-statues, there are [. . .] casters of models, two men; engravers of cast pieces, two men; inlayers, two men; stone sculptors, two men; statue-makers, two men; jewelers, two men; total, twelve men on monthly service, or forty-eight men in all. They are not consecrated to the god. They are the ones who bring into the world the *seshemu*-statues [. . .] As to the most secret work, [it is done] by servants consecrated to the gods, [chosen] from the prophets, cleansed by the purification of great ablution, who work when no eye can see them, under the authority of the overseer of secret rites, of the hierogrammat, of the divine father and chief lector priest. They [will go] to each chapel where it must be done, and from image to image, according to what is written in the sacred book as laid down by The-One-Who-Knows-the-Two-Lands [Thoth]."

Scene from the Deir al-Medina tomb of the sculptor Ipuy showing the making and consecrating of funerary furnishings

Once consecrated and placed in their respective chapels, royal and divine statues were ready to receive the daily worship that kept them alive in the earthly world for which they had been fashioned. They were then called by a special term that reveals the initiatory nature of these rites. The large dedicatory inscription left by Ramesses II in his father's temple at Abydos is enlightening on this subject. The young king, having realized that the building was still unfinished, discovered "his *seshem*-statue on the ground, not having been given birth as a *rekhenef*-statue in the Mansion of Gold." Similarly, in a Ramesside administrative papyrus, the king ordered that "high dignitaries bring a *rekhenef*-statue of *bekhen*-stone to [. . .] Egypt, so that it can be set in the Place of Truth, beside the temple of Usermaatre-Setepenre, the great god . . . [It was] left in the strong room of the Tomb where it remains half sculpted." Finally, a Twentieth Dynasty letter alludes to a sculptor ('one who gives birth to bodies of the gods')

Left:
Scene from the Theban tomb of Vizier Rekhmira, showing various types of royal statues leaving the workshop of the temple of Amun

Right:
Cult statue of King Amenhotep I in painted wood from Deir al-Medina (Musée du Louvre, Paris)

these practices were to the functioning of the pharaonic monarchy. The Dramatic Ramesseum Papyrus presents the ceremonies, probably devised during the reign of Amenemhat III, that evoke the burial and rebirth of the king over a statue of Sesostris I. A similar rite was documented in the second half of the second millennium BCE in the form of the ritual embarkation, every ten days, of the statue of Thutmose II, then that of Tutankhamun. Comparison could be made with worship of royal "statues of millions of years" that apparently began during the reign of Thutmose III.

Throughout Egypt, during every period, new forms of these liturgies blossomed in contexts both private and official. The "Mansion of millions of years," first mentioned toward the end of the Middle Kingdom, began to replace the "Mansion of *Ka*" and the old mortuary temples. They might be limited to one room, or to one part of the temple such as the hypostyle hall at Karnak, or else comprise vast buildings such as the temple of Sety I at Abydos, not to mention the temples on the west bank of Thebes during the Ramesside Period. They incarnated the liturgical potential of the old rites even as they adapted to new practices. Their increase generated, in turn, ceremonies that collectively incorporated successive beneficiaries of such worship: a scene in the temple of Sety I at Abydos described the litanies and "offerings given by the king" to ancestor kings, while the Akhmenu temple at Karnak included a room whose decoration was entirely devoted to the depiction of statues of Thutmose III's predecessor kings. Major regional festivities, such as the feast of Min, involved several processions led by the reigning king "escorted by statues of the deceased kings of Upper and Lower Egypt."

Despite an extraordinary accumulation in the temples of these sculptures of gods,

who was reproached for having "taken his friends to see the large *rekhenef*-statues at night, in the absence of chiefs, deputies, or administrators."

As we see, then, there was a rich vocabulary to describe various categories of statue. Right from the Old Kingdom, distinctions were made between statues for permanent worship (placed in the main shrine or in one of the chapels in a temple), from ritual statues (used only for special ceremonies), and from monumental statues (placed near the entrances and in the courts of sacred precincts). Whereas the number of royal portraits increased from the Fourth Dynasty onwards, few divine images prior to the New Kingdom have survived. Depending on the reign, five or six niches in the most sacred part of mortuary temples were reserved for statues of the king, while several hundred royal portraits of all kinds and all sizes have come to light during excavations of burial complexes. The largest were used for ceremonies that took place only on the spot where they stood, whereas ritual statues were the object of an everyday cult that treated them as living beings. Daily divine rituals were depicted in the decoration of Sety I's temple in Abydos and in several sacerdotal papyri. The ritual in royal mortuary temples of the

Old Kingdom, meanwhile, can be deduced from the archives of Neferirkare Kakai's temple at Abusir. The rite involved ablutions, purifications, anointments, and presentation of food and fabrics to the statues; it was performed twice a day. One after another, the niche-shrines were unsealed, opened, and then closed and re-sealed once the ceremony was over.

Worship of royal statues underwent extraordinary development over time. Coronation ceremonies, jubilee celebrations, and many other monarchic festivities provided occasions for producing royal and divine figures throughout the country. During the Old Kingdom, a royal institution called the "Mansion of *Ka*" linked a statue of the king to a holy shrine; then, under the Sixth Dynasty, this favor was extended, by royal decree, to members of the royal family and worthy high officials. Soon the king would even accord private individuals the boon of placing a statue of themselves on the outskirts, and later even inside, the sacred enclosure. A temple's open spaces were thereby steadily invaded by hundreds, indeed thousands, of sculptures. Even though just a minute fraction of the evidence of statue worship has survived, a few cases and various monumental groups suffice to demonstrate how crucial

kings, and simple mortals, destructions of various kinds, successive architectural renovations, and the need for each new monarch to spread his own image led to the elimination or disappearance of many of them. Some cult statues were stored very near the shrine, such as the golden-headed Horus of Nekhen and the bronze statues of Pepy I, found in a stone chest beneath the innermost shrine in the Thutmosid temple at Hierakonpolis. Others were placed in crypts, as at Dendera where it was once again the memory of Pepy I that was worshiped through a gold statue of the kneeling king presenting the young god Ihy to his mother, Hathor. The statue appeared not only in Hathor's chapel but also on a wall of one of the crypts, where the reasons for this devotion are explained: the plan of the temple was allegedly laid out during the reign of Thutmose III, thanks to the discovery "of ancient texts written on a leather scroll from the period of the Companions of Horus, found at Memphis in a chest at the royal palace, in the days of the King of Upper and Lower Egypt, Lord of the Two Lands Meryre, Son of Re, Lord of the Crowns Pepy, endowed with life, stability, and power, like Re, eternally." The statue was not a relic dating back to the Sixth Dynasty, however, but a votive piece made when the temple of Hathor was built.

A good number of royal cult statues were in fact produced at a greater or lesser interval after the death of the king, such pious acts being performed with a certain delay regardless of whether they were official, semi-official, or private in nature. Thus the temple of Hathor on the plateau of Serabit al-Khadim in Sinai contained statuettes of King Snefru and the monarchs who ordered expeditions to the turquoise mines during the Twelfth Dynasty. These portraits were placed there

by officials from the treasury charged with running the mines, in a chapel reserved for the monarchic rites associated with the goddess Hathor. Then there was the cult of Amenhotep I and his mother Ahmes-Nefertari, mainly attested during the Ramesside and Late Periods. Statuary cults engendered yet more statue worship, given the monarchs' desire to associate their own image to those of their most revered predecessors. The temple of Mentuhotep II at Deir al-Bahari provides a good example. As a re-unifier of Egypt at the end of the First Intermediate Period, Mentuhotep II soon came to be considered a particularly holy king, and his temple was a site of pilgrimage during the "Beautiful Festival of the Valley." Early in the Eighteenth Dynasty, Amenhotep I, who had apparently built a temple nearby, left a colossal statue there that was depicted on a stela beside the stela of Mentuhotep II.

Other pharaohs, notably Amenhotep III and above all Ramesses II, organized worship of their statues during their own lifetimes. Many records have survived at Karnak, Luxor, Memphis, and Pi-Ramesses of popular demonstrations around colossi of the king. On the stela of a military scribe we see the entire army express its fervor and enthusiasm for the king who distributes "money and all good things from the palace" as well as for the king's monumental image amid the thronging soldiers who run and leap while brandishing the gifts they have caught. Colossi became associated with a divine form whose name was reflected in part of their name, "Re-of-Monarchs," thereby playing an interceding role between humans and the world of the gods. In this way, such statues blithely assumed the epithet of "the ones who hear prayers."

Bronze statue of Pepy I or Merenre from a cache found in the temple of Hierakonpolis (Egyptian Museum, Cairo)

Far left:
Golden-headed Horus of Nekhen from a cache found in the temple of Hierakonpolis (Egyptian Museum, Cairo)

The Life and Death of Statues in the Temple

The worship of royal statues was not necessarily limited to mass cults around colossi. The seated statue of Mentuhotep II must have occupied a little shrine at the back of the hypostyle hall of his mortuary temple. Howard Carter found the statue shrouded in a piece of linen—as though it were the king's mortal remains—on the ground of a vaulted chamber of the underground corridor leading to a kind of cenotaph. Thanks to this unusual treatment, the sandstone sculpture, nearly two meters high and clearly made for a jubilee celebration (the king is wearing the short jubilee cloak), retained its original polychrome decoration. The black color of his skin indicated that the king was dead, as was often the case with two- and three-dimensional depictions of the god Osiris. The black face, pupils, beard, hands, legs, and cubic throne contrast strikingly with the white cloak and corneas and with the bright red crown of the North.

We might wonder at what period this transfer occurred. The temple of Deir al-Bahari was long a site of monarchic veneration and was only deconsecrated at a late date. But other statues, whose flesh was colored the red ocher of a living king, continued to populate this holy site, and it is possible that the sanctuary remained active even after people no longer had access to the real speos itself, or that the statue of the deceased king had been ritually buried and replaced by another. The discovery of foundation deposits, also wrapped in linen shrouds, under the four corners of the main part of the building might suggest a certain contemporaneousness of these practices. However, Édouard Naville's unearthing of a statue of Amun dating from the late Eighteenth Dynasty,

which had replaced an older statue, suggests the existence of other operations by New Kingdom monarchs who installed their mortuary temples as close as possible to that of Mentuhotep II. Such monarchs included Amenhotep I, Hatshepsut, and Thutmose III, who built a little sanctuary to Hathor in the first court of the temple.

Royal mortuary temples, various categories of monarchic chapels, and "Mansions of millions of years" usually dedicated to the memory of a single king—sometimes along with his father or mother—underwent few transformations while they were still active even though they suffered from looting and ruin once they were abandoned. It is therefore likely that whatever is left of their sculptural furnishing is relatively representative of the original arrangement of the monument. The same is not at all true with divine temples that were constantly renovated and rebuilt,

sometimes in radical fashion, from reign to reign. Whatever interest a pharaoh might have in a given predecessor and the ideological import of his reign, he could be inspired to move predecessors' statues to the benefit of a new architectural and sculptural program.

That was apparently the case with Ramesses II when he remodeled Amenhotep III's royal house of *ka* at Luxor. After the Amarna Period, when the names of the king and Amun were obliterated, Tutankhamun and Horemheb had the walls flanking the processional colonnade decorated with scenes showing the main sequences of the

Above:
View of the niche at the back of the hypostyle hall of the mortuary temple of Mentuhotep II

Right:
Polychrome statue of Mentuhotep II wearing his jubilee cloak (Egyptian Museum, Cairo)

Colossi of Amenhotep III and Ramesses II in the first court of the temple of Luxor

Indeed, the majority of those statues were made during the reigns of Amenhotep III, Tutankhamun, and Horemheb. Among the dated items, only two Ramesside statues in very poor condition and two Twenty-fifth Dynasty sculptures were deposited with that group. We are therefore led to wonder whether this cache was created when Ramesses II implemented his architectural program. The colossi of Amenhotep III would have been moved and re-inscribed with Ramesses' name in the new part of the temple, while statues of more modest dimensions would have been buried beneath the court built by Amenhotep III.

Depictions of statues on the walls of temples and tombs of high officials provide little information about their original location, except for the colossi placed at the entrance. Most of the pre–Nineteenth Dynasty statues in the cache are divine statues that could have been located in the secret parts of the temple. The portrait of Amenhotep III in the form of a liturgical statue of the king as Atum placed on a sledge constitutes a three-dimensional illustration of the confirmation of sovereignty that the king came to seek every year in the temple of royal ka during the feast of Opet. In this context, it may have been placed in the hypostyle hall that contained the decorative scenes of the same festival. The same is true of a sculpted pair showing the king kneeling and offering two round vases to Atum, and of two almost identical statues showing Amun transmitting the essence of royal power to Horemheb. These latter two must have been arranged symmetrically on either side of a temple circuit. Whereas the colossi at the entrance and the first court of the Ramesside temple were veritable cult statues still reserved for mass worship, this pair formed a kind of way-station between the ritual statues of the sovereign and those of the main gods,

festival of Opet. During the Nineteenth Dynasty, Ramesses II added a new peristyle court to the temple, plus a monumental pylon behind which Hatshepsut's triple shrine was rebuilt. In front of this façade (depicted in a relief in the first court) were erected two large obelisks flanked by several colossal statues. Most of the royal statues that remain in the temple today are of Ramesses II, except for several colossi of Amenhotep III usurped by Ramesses or his son, Merenptah. The statues set in front of the pylon—two seated colossi and two pairs of standing statues, were authentic sculptures of Ramesses II, as are the ones framing the entrance to the great colonnade. In the southern part of the first court, standing statues of Amenhotep III that Ramesses II had re-engraved with his own titulary are placed between the columns of the portico. They obviously came from previously constructed features—the old façade, colonnade, and peristyle court. Two grouped pairs of Amun and Mut, erected by Tutankhamun at the entrance to the colonnade, were also usurped by Ramesses II. Such a partisan approach suggests the possibility of a burial of the statues found in the cache at Luxor.

Left:
Sculpted group of Horemheb and Atum
from the cache found at Luxor

Right:
Sculpted group of Horemheb and Amun
from the cache found at Luxor

seen only by a select public that was allowed to enter farther into the temple yet did not have access to the naos, which was the sole prerogative of priests.

Given the nature of the caches at Doukki Gel and Gebel Barkal, it is beyond doubt that statues of the five different kings coexisted on those sites. Their stelae, too, at Kawa as well as Gebel Barkal, copied each other and existed side by side, and occasionally referred explicitly to previous reigns. It remains to be determined if the statues were spread throughout several buildings or assembled in a single spot on a given site. The existence of two distinct deposits at Gebel Barkal, combining fragments of statues of highly different dimensions, suggests that they might have been distributed between B 500 and B 800, indeed B 900. The fact that several of them are colossi between three and four meters tall offers a clue to their original placement. If we look at surviving Egyptian depictions, such colossi—whether seated or standing— generally flanked the main gateways of pylons, which would lead us to suggest that these statues stood before the façades

Above:
Relief on the temple of Luxor showing obelisks and colossi of Ramesses II as they were originally arrayed in front of the first pylon

Far right:
Relief from the portico of the festival hall of Thutmose IV at Karnak, showing various cult statues of the monarch

of contemporaneous buildings, especially since the sacred mountain would then have served as backdrop.

At Doukki Gel, two temples might have hosted these statues, because the pit where they were buried lay between the buildings, as mentioned above. The zone between the temples, in fact, seems to have been occupied by a coherent edifice that we are tempted to compare to an Egyptian Mansion of Gold, like the one at Karnak described above: the central part, comprising a colonnaded court, provided access to each of the two temples, as well as to the L-shaped room to the north and to a workshop to the south. We can be sure that this type of arrangement was known

to Kushite kings since one of the rare vestiges of a Mansion of Gold, located to the northeast of the hypostyle hall of the temple of Amun at Karnak, was the work of Shabaqo. At Doukki Gel, a cartouche of this same king was found on several blocks immediately next to the L-shaped room, in front of the eastern temple. By the New Kingdom, the workshop was endowed with round kilns fitted with a system of bellows. This installation was used for a very long time, since small bronze statues of deities and faience amulets were still being produced there at the end of the Meroitic era. On the other side of the court, a long storehouse ran along the wall of the L-shaped room, with which it

communicated via a narrow, concealed door. This type of structure is appropriate for storing precious materials or objects. The profusion of gold leaf found in part of the room and in the pit might be evidence of work related to the decoration and maintenance of liturgical objects.

The location and organization of the architectural ensemble between the two temples at Doukki Gel bears certain similarities to buildings at Gebel Barkal. The Kushite edifice to the northeast of B 500 has not yet been completely excavated, but we can see the paving of a fairly developed building, like that of Shabaqo at Karnak. Meanwhile, the outbuildings erected between B 800 and B 900 are

more explicit. They form a long narrow complex with a main room and a series of storehouses corresponding to the features of a Mansion of Gold. The depositing of the cache seems to have provoked major transformations, during which the room was enlarged at the expense of the second court of a temple rebuilt in stone during—or shortly after—the reign of Aspelta. This physical connection between what we propose to interpret as a Mansion of Gold and the cache does not, in itself, constitute a proof. However, the overall layout and, in particular, the proximity of these structures with the courtyards of the relevant temples lend added weight to the hypothesis. Work done posterior to the burying

of the broken statues also indicates a desire for a continuity transcending the destruction that probably accompanied the toppling of the royal portraits.

Like the Egyptian sculptures that inspired them, the statues at Doukki Gel bear traces of successive interventions on the surface of the stone, as discussed above. These traces, along with countless fragments of gold leaf and plaster, show that these images were not only painted and gilded in places, but also that their decoration was modified several times; additions of gilded stucco, glass, and lapis lazuli were probably applied as finery during special occasions. Their size makes it impossible to view these statues as shrine idols, but nothing prevents us from thinking that they were objects of worship. They "came to life" in the context of the rite of the opening of the mouth, like all ritual items, as shown on the reliefs of the Thutmose III's Mansion of Gold at Karnak, where we see, for example, the consecration of the *userhat* (sacred barque) of Amun and of two obelisks. This was also the case of statues of Thutmose IV depicted on the west wall of Thutmose's festival hall at Karnak, where the king simultaneously consecrates various objects and "monuments of gold and precious gems of all kinds."

Such evidence of regular maintenance and embellishment is consubstantial with the sacred nature of the Doukki Gel statues. The extraordinary condition of these statues at the moment they were dismembered is worth recalling, notably their high polish. This observation might constitute a crucial clue as to their location in the temple or temples. Indeed, the statue of Taharqa was almost one hundred years old when Psamtik II launched his military campaign. The appealing hypothesis of a position in front of the pylons therefore becomes difficult to defend in light of the fine surfaces. These statues would probably have been sheltered underneath the porticoes of the courtyards of the two temples equidistant from the cache. But it is hard to take this line of reasoning much further, since the surviving in situ vestiges of the two buildings correspond to renovations posterior to these events and hence to the deposit of the cache. The method and location of the deposits at both Gebel Barkal and Doukki Gel differ from comparable examples in Egypt and Sudan. The combination of a place of manufacture and consecration of statues with a kind of cemetery of said statues is not at all apparent in the other caches, which were of course located on ground that was sacred yet usually open, probably for convenience, such as the so-called "Cour de la Cachette" at Karnak and the second courtyard of Luxor temple. In contrast, at both Doukki Gel and Gebel Barkal the burial took place in relatively narrow, hard-to-reach rooms. If we accept the idea that these were Houses of Gold, however, then it is easy to acknowledge that specialized teams would have been accustomed to such transfers.

The condition of the various fragments and their deliberate arrangement in the pit indicate that the statues were handled with great care by men familiar with similar tasks and perhaps dismayed by the state of the venerable objects that had once been in their care. Should we view this operation as a kind of ritual burial of broken statues or simply the work of clearing the temple after the battles described in the Shellal stela? While the state of the cache does not match the treatment lavished on the jubilee statue of Mentuhotep II beneath his mortuary temple at Deir al-Bahari, it is nevertheless a long way from a simple dump. The presence of several other pits in the same room where this *favissa* was dug suggests that such practices recurred before and after the reign of Aspelta. One also thinks of the amazing burial of Egyptian royal and private statues in the last tumuli of Classic Kerma, just a few kilometers away. These various cases underscore the magical quality that Kerma monarchs—followed by Nubian pharaohs—attributed to Egyptian royal statues (and, later, 'Egyptian-style' royal statues). What counted was not just the statues' glamorous monarchic content, but also their role as intercessors between the divine world and the earthly one. Whether the L-shaped room was part of a veritable Mansion of Gold or some other category of chapel, the broken statues continued to benefit from the rites performed there. It is therefore our task to restore them and offer them the homage, if not the worship, they deserve in the new museum at Kerma where they will shortly be placed on display.

Epilogue

In every era Egyptians took their models from the past. Kings carried out or ordered searches of the archives in order to remain as faithful as possible to the works of the ancients. When a Thirteenth Dynasty king, Neferhotep I, wanted to make a new statue of the god Osiris, he expressed the desire to "consult writings from the primordial days of Atum," because, he claimed, "if I know the form of the god, I will have him depicted as he was originally." Canons remained extremely stable for most of the country's history, despite an undeniable ability to innovate. When the Kushite kings of the Twenty-fifth Dynasty took over the royal workshops, artists drew their main inspiration from sculptures and reliefs dating back the Old and Middle Kingdoms. Their Saite successors would do the same. Of course, everyone brought to their respective output a uniqueness that distinguished it from the antiquities they imitated. Nevertheless, it is possible in certain cases to identify the precise sources they relied upon. The phenomenon was current not only within Egypt itself, but extended quickly to all of Nubia, which, as far as Twenty-fifth Dynasty kings were concerned, was thereafter one with Egypt.

Throughout that period and even after, striking evidence has survived of the importation into Kush of Egyptian institutions, religious and monarchic practices, and elaborate funerary compositions that steadily helped to enrich indigenous institutions, practices, and beliefs, creating new intellectual and artistic foci, as convincingly demonstrated by royal titularies. Right from the start of this period we see the name of Alara, considered the defining ancestor of the new line, written inside a cartouche on the stela of his daughter Tabiry, the great wife of Piankhy; while on

The Horus name of Senkamanisken on the back pillar of one of his statues

The temple of Amun at Meroe

the Kawa stela dated year 6, Taharqa preceded Alara's name with the title "son of Re." Meanwhile Kashta, the founder of the actual dynasty, was given an Egyptian-like throne name in addition to his Nubian birth name, both being inscribed in cartouches. Following them, the veritable masters of Egypt and Sudan were endowed with complete titularies in the most orthodox manner. Adopting habits begun in Egypt during the Third Intermediate Period, monarchs delved back into the names of the most famous pharaohs to compose their own titularies, with the exception of the birth name, which remained Kushite. The royal statues made for Nubian temples, like the temples

themselves, thereafter reproduced these royal titularies according to the conventional rules.

Even after Tanutamun lost control of Egypt, his successors continued to style themselves as pharaohs. Indeed, they almost never referred to their realm on Sudanese territory, but constantly invoked a purely virtual dominion over Egypt. It should be remembered that even during the Twenty-fifth Dynasty this dominion was never exercised easily or uninterruptedly, for the Kushite kings had to reconquer all or part of Egypt several times. That is probably why Tanutamun's defeat was not perceived as final, but rather as an unfortunate episode in a long and turbulent history. It is therefore less surprising to witness the strict application of institutional practices that had lost their original content.

Whereas the back pillar on the statue of Taharqa includes only his two main names, and those on the statues of Tanutamun add just the Horus name to the first two, the back pillars of the sculptures of Senkamanisken, Anlamani, and Aspelta list all five names, conspicuously invoking a dominion they have totally lost. Also noteworthy is the presence of the crown of Upper and Lower Egypt on two of the statues, the presence of the double uraeus on all of them, and the horns of Amun on Anlamani's (which makes this Napatan monument the sole surviving three-dimensional example of this divine Egyptian attribute on the head of a king).

In the administrative sphere, the Napatan kingdom was divided into nomes, in imitation of Egypt, according to Anlamani's Coronation Stela. We know little of the organization of the Nubian court after its retreat to Napata, and the use of the title *kur* in the Tanis version of Psamtik

II's stela to refer to the Nubian monarch would seem to imply a political structure unrelated to the pharaonic state. This African title, for that matter, would resurface in the second demotic tale of Setne Khaemwas who described a magic joust between the king of Egypt and his Meroitic counterpart. Several stelae of Aspelta invoke Napatan officials who bear the Egyptian titles for 'commander,' 'overseer of sealed palace objects,' 'overseer of Granary,' and 'royal scribe,' but their use seems adapted to a reality quite different from the Egyptian system. Later, it would be the oldest texts in cursive Meroitic script, dating from the first century BCE, that revealed the presence at the head of Meroe's government of a *psenti* (the Egyptian term for minister of economy since Saite days) as well as the existence of various borrowings from Egyptian administrative vocabulary, such as the term 'general,' which also took on a new meaning. These details point to the survival of multiple contacts between the two countries from Psamtik II's campaign to the emergence of the new African kingdom.

As far as royal iconography goes, the panther skin that was the special garb of the *sem* priest became an important element of regalia in Napatan and later Meroitic art, although pertaining to rites that differed from Egyptian customs. Yet the statue of Aspelta's successor, Aramatelqo, from Napata, still reproduces the exact model of the Egyptian sovereign wearing the festive jubilee garment. In liturgical texts as well as iconography, important vestiges of the old models survived, alongside the development of an original civilization that also sought inspiration from other Mediterranean sources. Even though its capital moved farther south, the new kingdom would not lose touch with the contemporary world. It is strange to discover a multicultural art where the image of Egypt remained ubiquitous but where Greek and Roman influences were constantly growing. Above all, the African features that have been occasionally noted in the modeling of a sphinx or a series of *shabtis* toward the middle of the first millennium BCE would progressively assert themselves until they became a determining trait of Meroitic sculpture.

Aerial view of the last pyramids to be built at Gebel Barkal

APPENDICES

Chronology

PERIOD	EGYPT
Paleolithic (1,000,000–9000 BCE)	Nag Ahmed al-Khalifa, Nazlet Kahter, Nazlet Safaha, Wadi Kubbaniya
Mesolithic (9000–6000 BCE)	Elkabian, Nabata Playa, Bir Kiseiba, Fayum B
Neolithic (6000–3500 BCE)	Merimda, al-Omari Beni Salame, Fayum A, Badari
Predynastic (3500–2950 BCE)	Maadi, Buto, Nagada, al-Amrah, Hierakonopolis, Adaima
Thinite Period (2950–2780 BCE) Recent pre-Kerma	Unification of Upper and Lower Egypt
Old Kingdom (2635–2140 BCE) 3rd–6th Dynasties	Zoser, Snefru, Khufu, Khafra Tety, Pepy I, Pepy II
First Intermediate Period (2140–2020 BCE) 8th Dynasty, early 9th Dynasty	Breakdown of territorial unity; several parallel dynasties
Middle Kingdom (2022–1750 BCE) Late 9th Dynasty to 13th Dynasty	Reunification of Egypt
Second Intermediate Period (1750–1550 BCE) Late 13th Dynasty to 17th Dynasty	The Hyksos occupy the eastern Delta; Egyptian kingdom limited to area around Thebes.
New Kingdom (1550–1080 BCE) 18th to 20th Dynasty	Thutmosids, Amenhotep IV (Akhenaten), Ramessids
Third Intermediate Period (1080–715 BCE) 21st Dynasty to 24th Dynasty	Power divided between North and South; several parallel dynasties 736 BCE: Piankhy's Victory Stele; conquest of Upper and Middle Egypt
Late Period (715–330 BCE) 25th Dynasty to 30th Dynasty	715 BCE: Shabaqo conquers Lower Egypt 690: Taharqa ascends the throne 674: Esarhaddon captures Memphis 664: Nekau I dies, Psamtik I and Tanutamun come to power 663: Thebes sacked by the Assyrians 656: Psamtik I reunites Upper and Lower Egypt Names of 25th Dynasty pharaohs erased by Psamtik II 525: Cambyses conquers Egypt 389: Nephrites I liberates Egypt 341: Artaxerxes re-conquers Egypt
Greek Period (330–30 BCE)	330 BCE: Alexander conquers Egypt
Roman Period (30 BCE onward)	30 BCE: Octavian conquers Egypt, which becomes a Roman province 392 CE: Theodosius outlaws paganism

NUBIA	KERMA
Arkin, Sai, Gebel Sahaba	Kabrinarti lower paleolithic Epipaleolithic
Shamarkian, Early Khartoum, Khartoum variant	al-Barga mesolithic
Nubian neolithic (Kadruka, Selim basin) Khartoum neolithic	al-Barga neolithic Eastern necropolis neolithic
Group A, al-Kadada	Old and middle pre-Kerma
	Recent pre-Kerma
Egyptian expeditions Group C	Old Kerma (2450–2050 BCE) 2400: founding of Nubian town of Kerma with religious precinct
Group C	Old Kerma
Lower Nubia annexed; border extended to second cataract; forts built	Middle Kerma (2050–1750 BCE) Royal palaces, audience chamber Founding of a second city Large princely tumuli
Alliance between Hyksos and Kushites; Kerma monarchs occupy forts on second cataract	Classic Kerma (1750–1450 BCE) Construction of Deffufa Great royal tumuli and funerary temples
Nubia conquered beyond the fourth cataract, as far as Hagar al-Merwa; establishment of viceroyalty of Kush	1500 BCE: end of Kerma kingdom and foundation of Egyptian city of Pnubs on site of Doukki Gel, 1km north of Nubian town Thutmosid, Amarnian, and Ramessid temples
Several independent but Egyptianized Kushite kingdoms; scant Egyptian documentation; contacts maintained between Egypt and Nubia	
Kushite kingdom of Egypt and Nubia	Shabaqo's temple Taharqa's statue Tanutamun's statues
653 BCE: start of Napatan Dynasty (Atlanersa, Anlamani, Aspelta, Aramatelqo, Irike-Amanote) 400 BCE: start of Meroitic kingdom (Harsiotef, Akhratan)	Statues of Senkamanisken, Anlamani, Aspela 593 BCE: Psamtik II's campaign in Egypt Destruction of statues at Kerma and Gebel Barkal Napatan temples at Doukki Gel Town extends toward river
Nastasen, Arkamani I, etc.	
Amanishakheto, Natakamani, Amanitore ca. 400 CE: end of Meroitic kingdom	Meroitic temples at Doukki Gel

Bibliography

Ahmed, S. Eldin M. 1992. *L'agglomération napatéenne de Kerma: Enquête archéologique et ethnographique en milieu urbain*, Paris: Éditions Recherche sur les Civilisations.

Barguet, A ed. 1964. *Hérodote, L'enquête, Historiens grecs I*. Paris: Bibliothèque de la Pléiade.

Barguet, P. 1962. *Le temple d'Amon-Rê à Karnak: Essai d'exégèse, Recherches d'Archéologie, de Philologie et d'Histoire* 21. Cairo: Institut Français d'Archéologie Orientale.

Barguet, P., J. Leclant, and C. Robichon. 1954. *Karnak-Nord IV, Fouilles de l'Institut Français d'Archéologie Orientale* 25. Cairo: Institut Français d'Archéologie Orientale.

Bell, L. 1985. "Luxor Temple and the Cult of the Royal Ka," *Journal of Near Eastern Studies* 44. Chicago.

Bell, L., W. Murnane, *et al.* 1992. *Louxor, temple du Ka royal*. Dijon: Éditions Faton.

Blackman, A.M. 1937. "Preliminary Report on the Excavations at Sesebi, Northern Province, Anglo-Egyptian Sudan, 1936–37," *Journal of Egyptian Archaeology* 23. London.

Bonnet, C. 1986. *Kerma, territoire et métropole: Quatre leçons au Collège de France*. Cairo: Institut Français d'Archéologie Orientale.

———. 1999. "The Funerary Traditions of Middle Nubia," *Eighth International Conference for Meroitic Studies, London, July 1996, British Museum Occasional Papers* 31. London.

Bonnet, C. and D. Valbelle. 2000. "Les sanctuaires de Kerma du Nouvel Empire à l'époque méroïtique," *Comptes Rendus de l'Académie des Inscriptions et Belles-Lettres*. Paris: Diffusion de Boccard.

———. 2003. "Un dépôt de statues royales du début du VIe siècle av. J.-C. à Kerma," *Comptes Rendus de l'Académie des Inscriptions et Belles-Lettres*. Paris: Diffusion de Boccard.

Bonnet, C., D. Valbelle, *et al.* 2000. *Edifices et rites funéraires de Kerma*. Paris: Errance.

———. 2004. *Le temple principal et le quartier religieux de Kerma*. Paris: Errance.

Bonnet, C. et al. "Fouilles archéologiques à Kerma, Soudan," *Genava* (new series) no. 26 (1978), no.

28 (1980), no. 30 (1982), no. 32 (1984), no. 34 (1986), no. 36 (1988), no. 39 (1991), no. 41 (1993), no. 43 (1995), no. 45 (1997), no. 47 (1999), no. 49 (2001), no. 51 (2003).

———. *Kerma, Royaume de Nubie*. Geneva, 1990.

Borger, R. 1956. *Die Inschriften Asarhaddons, Beiheft des Archivs für Orientforschung* 9. Graz: Im Selbstverlage des Herausgebers.

———. 1996. *Beiträge zum Inschriftenwerk Assurbanipals*. Wiesbaden: Harrassowitz.

Breyer, F. 2003. *Tanutamani: Die Traumstele und ihr Umfeld, Ägypten und altes Testament* 57. Wiesbaden: Harrassowitz.

Daumas, F. 1953. "Le trône d'une statuette de Pépi Ier trouvé à Dendara," *Bulletin de l'Institut Français d'Archéologie Orientale* 52. Cairo.

———. 1980. "Quelques textes de l'atelier des orfèvres dans le temple de Dendara." *Livre du centenaire 1880–1980, Mémoires de l'Institut Français d'Archéologie Orientale* 104. Cairo.

Derchain, P. 1990. "L'atelier des orfèvres à Dendera et les origines de l'alchimie," *Chronique d'Égypte* 130. Brussels.

Der Manuelian, P. 1994. *Living in the Past: On Archaism of the Egyptian Twenty-sixth Dynasty*. London/New York: Kegan Paul International.

Dunham, D. 1950. *The Royal Cemeteries of Kush, I: El Kurru*. Cambridge, Mass: Harvard University Press.

———. 1955. *The Royal Cemeteries of Kush II: Nuri*. Cambridge, Mass: Museum of Fine Arts, Boston.

———. 1970. *The Barkal Temples*. Boston: Museum of Fine Arts.

Eide, T., T. Hägg, R.H. Pierce, and L. Török. 1994. *Fontes historiae nubiorum: Textual Sources for the History of the Middle Nile Region between the Eighth Century BC and the Sixth Century AD I, From the Eighth to the Mid-Fifth Century BC*. Bergen: University of Bergen.

Gabolde, L. and M. Gabolde. 1989. "Les temples 'mémoriaux' de Thoutmosis II et Toutankhamon, un rituel destiné à des statues sur barques," *Bulletin de l'Institut Français d'Archéologie Orientale* 89. Cairo.

Goyon, J.-C. 1972. *Rituels funéraires de l'ancienne Égypte*. Paris: Les éditions du Cerf.

Goyon, J.C., C. Cardin, *et al.* 2004. *Trésors d'Égypte: La "cachette" de Karnak*. Grenoble: Musée Dauphinois.

Gratien, B. 1978. *Les cultures Kerma: Essai de classification*. Lille: Publications de l'université de Lille III.

Grimal, N. 1981. *La stèle triomphale de Pi'ankhy au Musée du Caire, Mémoires de l'Institut Français d'Archéologie Orientale* 105. Cairo: Publications de l'Institut Français d'Archéologie Orientale.

———. 1981. *Quatre stèles napatéennes au Musée du Caire, Mémoires de l'Institut Français d'Archéologie Oriental* 106. Cairo: Publications de l'Institut Français d'Archéologie Orientale.

Habachi, L. 1969. *Features of the Deification of Ramesses II, Abhandlungen des Deutschen Archäologischen Instituts Kairo* 5. Glückstadt: J. J. Augustin.

Hinkel, F. *et al.* 2001. *The Archaelogical Map of the Sudan: Supplement I.1. Der Tempelkomplex Meroe 250*. Berlin: Verlag Monumenta Sudanica.

Honegger, M. 2001. "Évolution de la société dans le bassin de Kerma, Soudan, des derniers chasseurs-cueilleurs au premier royaume," *Bulletin de la Société Française d'Égyptologie* 152. Paris.

Kendall, T., 1996. "Fragments Lost and Found: Two Kushite Objects Augmented," *Studies in Honor of William Kelly Simpson* II. Boston: Museum of Fine Arts.

Kitchen, K.A. 1973. *The Third Intermediate Period in Egypt, 1160–650 BC*. Warminster: Aris & Phillips Ltd.

Lauffray, J., S. Sauneron, and C. Traunecker. 1975. "La tribune du quai de Karnak et sa favissa," *Karnak V, 1970–1972*. Cairo.

Leclant, J. 1961. *Montouemhat, quatrième prophète d'Amon, prince de la ville, Bibliothèque d'Étude* 35. Cairo: Imprimerie de l'Institut Français d'Archéologie Orientale.

———. 1965. *Recherches sur les Monuments thébains de la XXVe dynastie dite Ethiopienne, Bibliothèque d'Étude* 36. Cairo: Institut français d'archéologie Orientale.

———. 1985. "Taharqa" and "Tanoutamon," *Lexikon der Ägyptologie* VI. Wiesbaden.

———. 1989–90. "Réflexions sur l'architecture égyptienne: règles et singularités," *Annuaire du Collège de France*. Paris.

Leclant, J. (ed). 1978–80. *Le monde Egyptien, les pharaons I-III*. Paris: Gallimard.

Leclant, J. and J. Yoyotte. 1952. "Notes d'histoire et de civilisation Ethiopiennes," *Bulletin de l'Institut Français d'Archéologie Orientale* 51. Cairo.

Letellier, B. 1991. "Thoutmosis IV à Karnak: hommage tardif rendu à un bâtisseur malchanceux," *Bulletin de la Société Française d'Égyptologie* 122. Paris.

Macadam, M.F.L. 1949–55. *The Temples of Kawa* I-II. London: Oxford University Press.

Maystre, C., C. Bonnet, *et al*. 1986. *Tabo I: Statue en bronze d'un roi méroïtique, Musée National de Khartoum, inv. 24705*. Geneva.

Moret, A. 1902. *Le rituel du culte divin journalier en Égypte*. Paris: E. Leroux.

Morkot, R.G. 2000. *The Black Pharaohs: Egypt's Nubian Rulers*. London: The Rubicon Press.

Posener-Kriéger, P. 1976. *Les archives du temple funéraire de Néferirkarê-Kakaï I-II, Bibliothèque d'Étude* 69. Cairo: Institut Français d'Archéologie Orientale.

Pritchard, J.B. 1969 (3rd edition). *Ancient Near Eastern Texts Relating to the Old Testament*. Princeton: Princeton University Press.

Privati, B. 1999. "La céramique de la nécropole orientale de Kerma, Soudan: essai de classification," *Cahier de Recherches de l'Institut de Papyrologie et d'Égyptologie de Lille* 20. Lille.

Reisner, G.A. 1917–20. "The Barkal Temples in 1916," *Journal of Egyptian Archaeology* 4 (1917), 5 (1918), 6 (1920).

———. 1923. "Excavations at Kerma, Parts I-V," *Harvard African Studies* 5-6. Cambridge, Mass.

Russmann, E.R., 1974. *The Representation of the King in the XXVth Dynasty, Monographie Reine Élisabeth* 3. Brussels: Fondation égyptologique Reine Elisabeth.

El-Saghir, M. 1992. *La découverte de la cachette des statues du temple de Louxor*. Mainz: P. von Zabern.

Sauneron, S. and J. Yoyotte., 1952. "La campagne nubienne de Psammétique II et sa signification historique," *Bulletin de l'Institut Français d'Archéologie Orientale* 50.

Schiff Giorgini, M. *et al*. 1998–2003. *Soleb* III-V. Cairo: Institut Français d'Archéologie Orientale.

Sethe, K. 1959. *Dramatische Texte zu altägyptischen Mysterienspielen, Untersuchungen zur Geschichte und Altertumskunde Ägyptens* 10. Berlin: J.C. Hinrichs'sche Buchhandlung.

Spalinger, A. 1978. "The Concept of the Monarchy during the Saite Epoch — An Essay of Synthesis," *Orientalia* 47.

———. 1982. "Psammetichus I " and "Psammetichus II," *Lexikon der Ägyptologie* IV. Wiesbaden.

Török, L. 1997. *Meroe City, an Ancient African Capital: John Garstang's Excavations in the Sudan*. London.

Traunecker, C. 1989. "Le 'Château de l'Or' de Thoutmosis III et les magasins nord du temple d'Amon," *Cahier de Recherches de l'Institut de Papyrologie et d'Égyptologie de Lille* 11.

Valbelle, D. 1998. *Histoire de l'État pharaonique*. Paris: Presses Universitaires de France.

———. 2003. "L'Amon de Pnoubs," *Revue d'Égyptologie* 54. Paris.

———. 2004. "The cultural significance of iconographic and epigraphic data found in the kingdom of Kerma" in T. Kendall, ed., *Nubian*

Studies 1998: Proceedings of the Ninth Conference of the International Society of Nubian Studies. Boston: Department of African-American Studies, Northeastern University, Boston.

Valbelle, D. and C. Bonnet. 1996. *Le sanctuaire d'Hathor, maîtresse de la turquoise: Sérabit el-Khadim au Moyen Empire*. Paris: Picard Editeur.

Vercouttter, J. 1961. "Le sphinx d'Aspelta de Defeia," *Mélanges Auguste Mariette, Bibliothèque d'Étude* 32. Cairo: Institut Français d'Archéologie Orientale.

Vercoutter, J., J. Leclant, F. M. Snowden, and J. Desanges. 1976. *L'image du noir dans l'art occidental I: Des pharaons à la chute de l'empire romain*. Paris: Bibliothèque des arts.

Welsby, D. A. 1986. *The Kingdom of Kush*. London: British Museum Press.

Welsby, D. A. and J. R. Anderson. 2004. *Sudan: Ancient Treasures*. London: The British Museum Press.

Wenig, S. 1978. *Africa in Antiquity: The Arts of Ancient Nubia and the Sudan*. Brooklyn: The Brooklyn Museum.

Wildung, D. 1984. *L'âge d'or de l'Égypte: Le Moyen Empire*. Freiburg: Presses Universitaires de France.

Wildung, D. (ed). 1997. *Soudan: Royaumes sur le Nil*. Paris: Institut du Monde Arabe.

Yoyotte, J. 1951. "Le martelage des noms royaux éthiopiens par Psammétique II," *Revue d'Égyptologie* 8. Paris.

———. 1958. "Néchao," *Dictionnaire de la Bible, Supplément VI*. Paris.

———. 1965. "Égypte ancienne," *Histoire universelle des origines à l'Islam I*. Paris : Gallimard.

———. 1989. "Le nom du 'Ministre de l'économie' de Saïs à Méroé," *Comptes Rendus de l'Académie des Inscriptions et Belles-Lettres*. Paris.

Photographic Credits

Acknowledgments

This book is directly related to the excavations that the University of Geneva's Mission Archéologique has been carrying out in Sudan for over thirty years, and as such it has benefited from much assistance.

Firstly, thanks go to Salah Eldin Mohamed Ahmed, who directed operations at the Doukki Gel site right from the start and who continues to be personally committed to this research program despite the other, major responsibilities that he has now assumed.

Equally valuable has been the unflagging support of the various directors of Sudan's Antiquities Department, in particular Hassan Hussein Idriss.

The quality of site drawings and visual documentation should be credited to Marion Berti, Marc Bundi, Gérard Deuber, Thomas Kohler, Alain Peillex, and Françoise Plojoux-Rochat, not forgetting Alfred Hidber, Béatrice Privati, and Philippe Ruffieux.

We would also like to thank all the photographers who have worked, in turn, at Kerma: Nicolas Faure who, under extremely difficult conditions, managed to do justice to the outstanding artistic qualities of these sculptures; Pascale Rummler-Kohler, who took many of the photos published here; and Daniel Berti and Jean-Baptiste Sevette.

Several friends have generously supplied us with many additional illustrations for the chapters on Egypt and other Sudanese sites. Our thanks naturally go to Abd el-Rahman Ali Mohamed, Philippe Brissaud, Renée Colardelle, Rita Freed, François Gourdon, Jean-François Gout, Tim Kendall, François Larché, Alain Lecler, Peter Der Manuelian, Alessandro Roccati, Vincent Rondot, Derek Welsby, Dietrich Wildung, and Jean-Michel Yoyotte.

Acknowledgments also go to Patricia Berndt, Nora Ferrero, and François Le Saout for their contribution to our work. Finally, we would like to stress the faithful support of Michel Valloggia in insuring the continuity of this scholarly program. The University of Geneva's Mission Archéologique in Sudan, headed since the 2002-2003 season by Matthieu Honegger, is funded by Switzerland's Fonds National de la Recherche Scientifique, by Geneva's Musée d'Art et d'Histoire, and by various private donors.

Note
The photographs having been taken at different times of the day,
the statues sometimes appear in different tones. The photographs
are reproduced exactly as they were taken, with the variations
due to the natural light.

First published in English in 2006 by
The American University in Cairo Press
113 Sharia Kasr el Aini, Cairo, Egypt
420 Fifth Avenue, New York, NY 10018
www.aucpress.com

Published by arrangement with Editions Citadelles & Mazenod

Translated from the French by Deke Dusinberre

ISBN-10: 977 416 010 X
ISBN-13: 978 977 416 010 3
Dar el Kutub No. 23747/05

Designed by Richard Medioni
Printed in Spain